AF372094

Andrea Polli

with an essay by
Philip R. S. Johnson

# HACK THE GRID

Hillman Photography Initiative

Carnegie Museum of Art
Pittsburgh, Pennsylvania

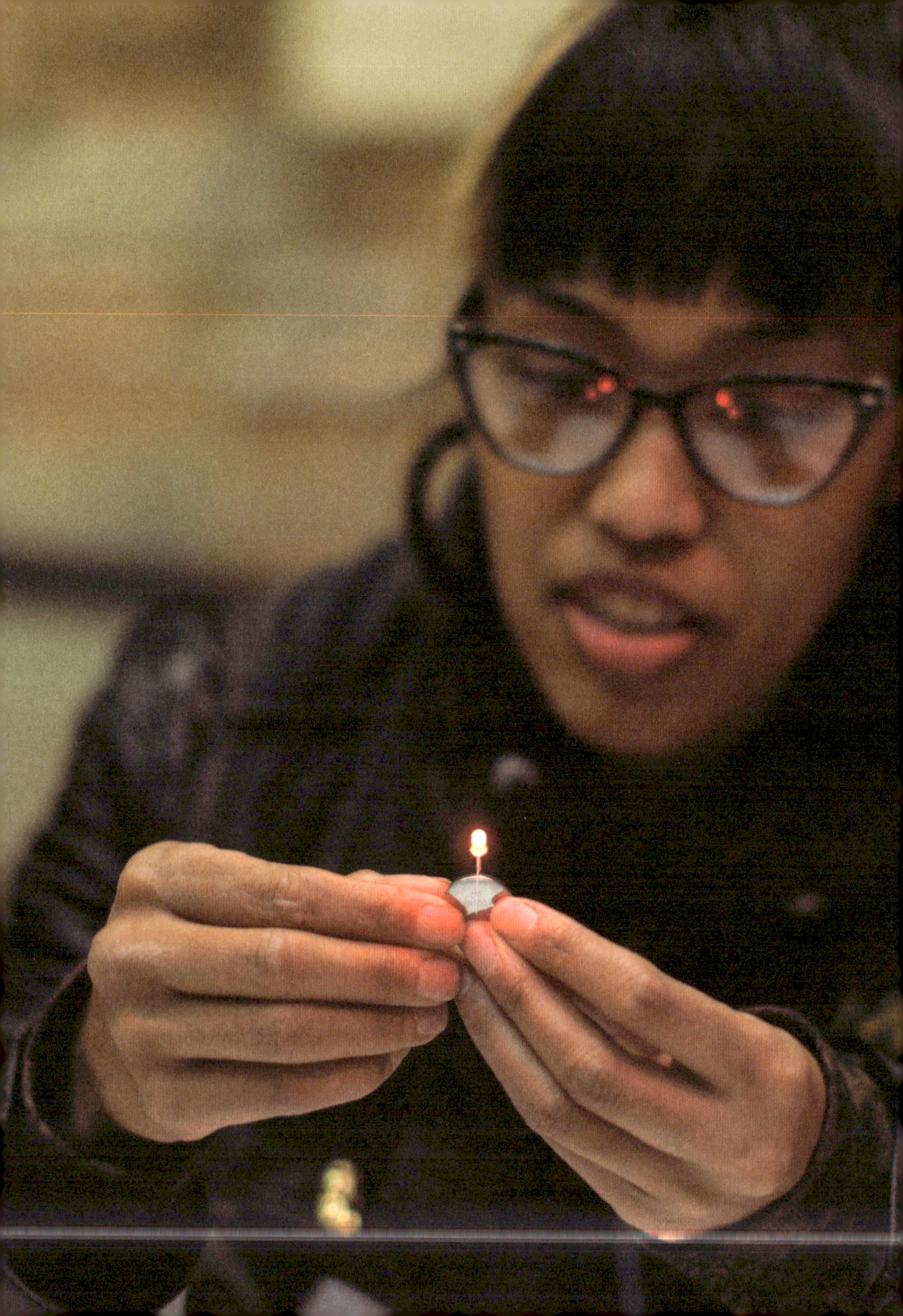

Welcome to *Hack the Grid*, a book and a movement that embraces the notion of "hacking" as learning through remaking. To "hack," as we define it, is to take something readily available and reconfigure it—realizing new questions, uses, and representations along the way. It is to understand something from the inside out. In short, it is to make something your own. We are neither advocating nor discussing the kind of online hacking that promotes theft, fear, instability, or destruction. Rather, our hacking is creative and generative; it is an action in the service of knowledge, cultural production, and civic engagement. Our goal for *Hack the Grid* is to foster a greater understanding about the energy you consume. Through this, you can make energy your own by experimenting with energy-related technologies and creating images as a means to explore new ideas. You can also make more informed choices about energy use and advocate for the kind of energy that you want in your homes and communities. Let's begin to hack the grid. This is our manifesto.

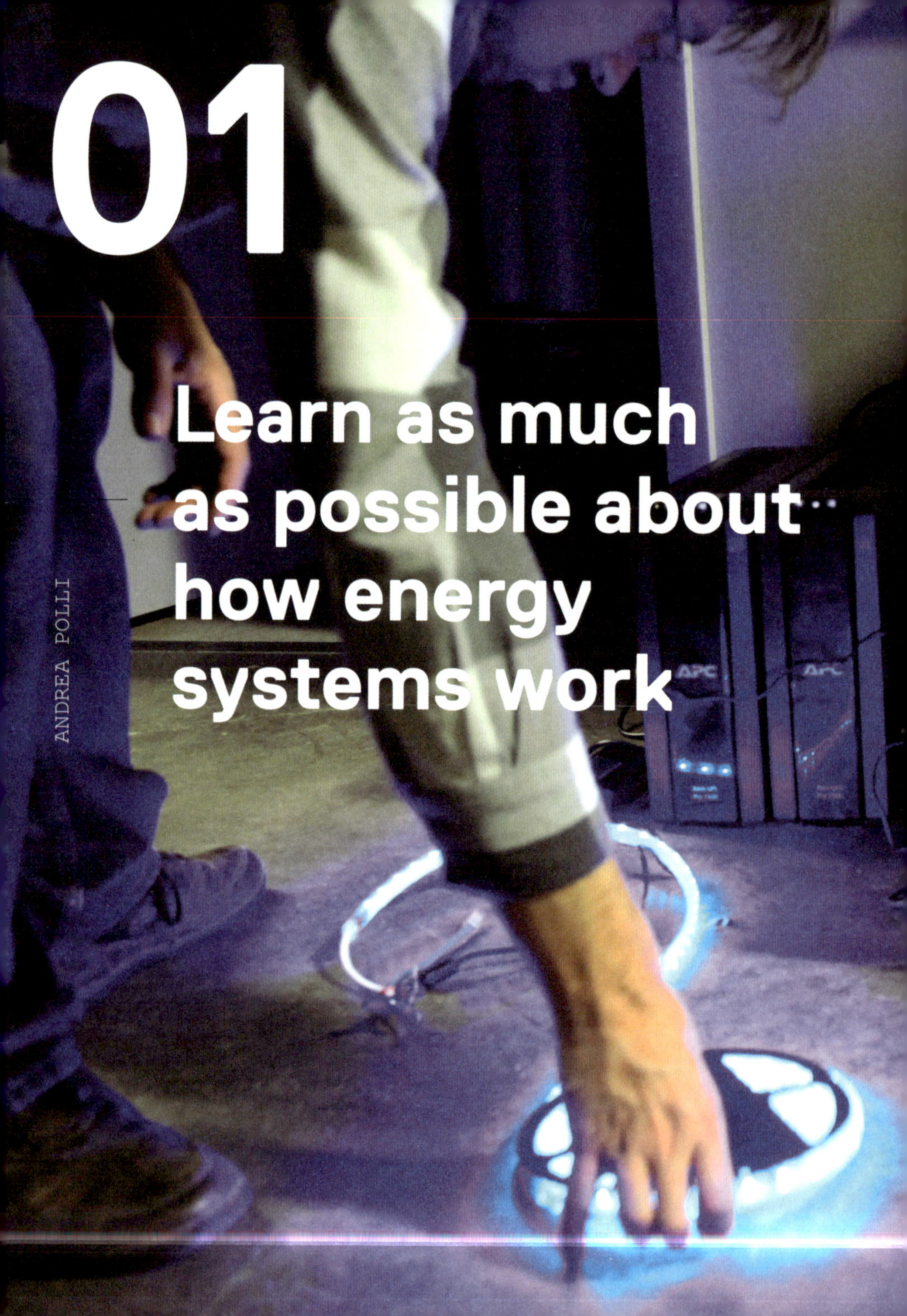
01
Learn as much
as possible about
how energy
systems work
ANDREA POLLI
APC
APC

We plug our devices into the wall and, almost magically, power is available to us. We don't have to think about where that power is coming from or where it is made. We are sure it will always be there, the same as the sun rises every day. But the process of getting power to that plug involves millions of choices. Material choices of wiring, fasteners, shielding, and coatings. Structural choices about where and how those wires move through space to distribute the energy. Design choices from where a power plug should be located to how the entire system is configured, monitored, and repaired. Most of these choices involve government regulation, and over the years the requirements have had to become increasingly layered. These regulations are designed to keep us safe from dangers like fire or electrocution, but what about less immediate dangers? Shouldn't we also look at the safety of our air and water over longer time spans? It's not an easy problem, and we need your brain power—and that of everyone who consumes energy— to solve it.

# 02

# Know how much energy you consume and its environmental impact

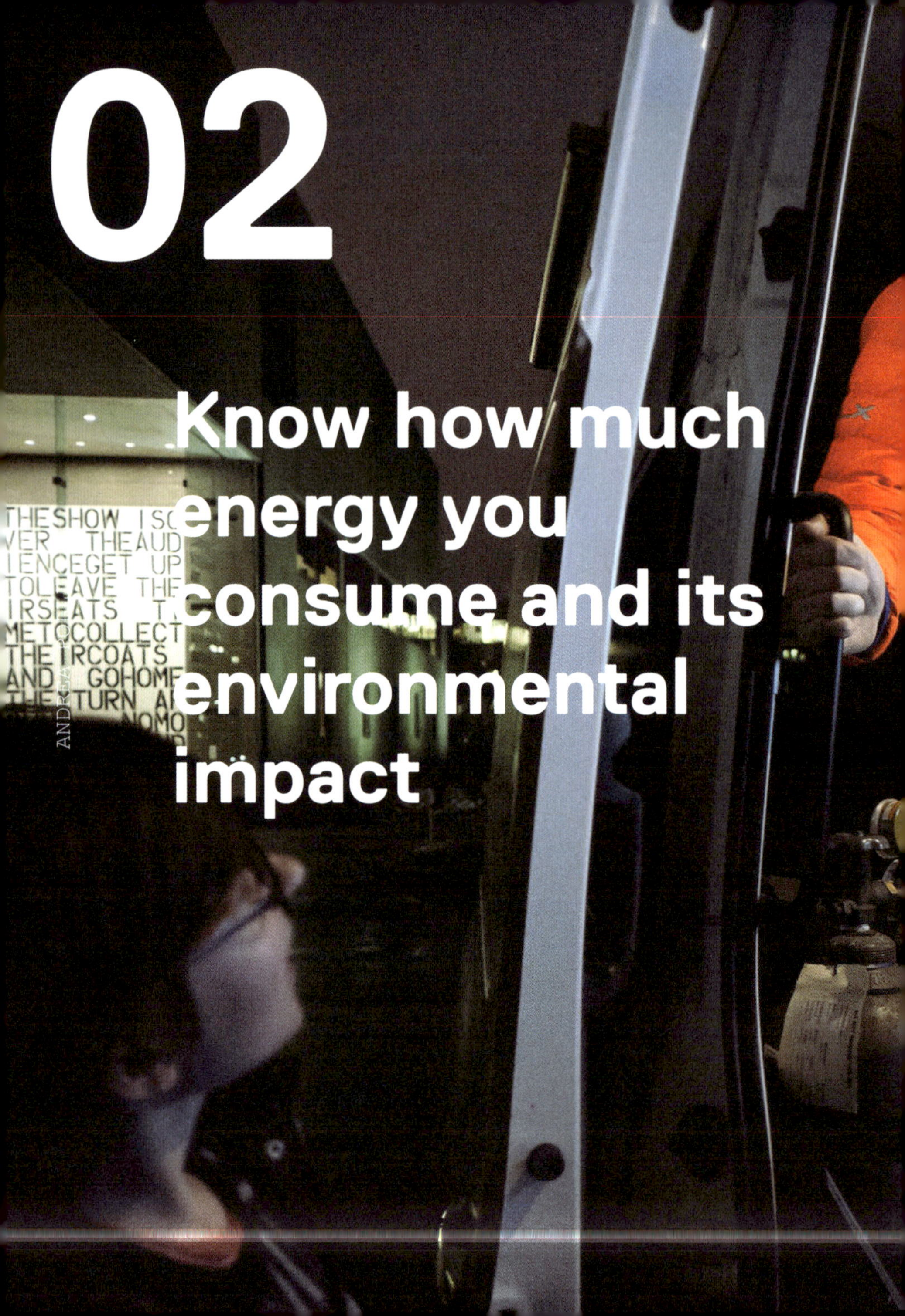

We have access today to information about every calorie we consume, and we can even separate "good" calories from "bad" calories. We know what fuels our bodies, and how our bodies respond to that fuel. We have apps that count every step we take. We can obtain readouts of our heart rate, and we can research with relative ease the most efficient ways to keep ourselves healthy. Why don't we do the same with our energy consumption? Environmental impacts from the energy production that powers our homes, vehicles, and devices affect our lives and our health— from the air we breathe to the water we drink to the food we eat. In many ways, the impacts of our own energy consumption may have a greater effect on us than the calories we consume and burn.

# 03

Demand that energy providers tell you the source of the energy you purchase

ANDREA POLLI

[1] John Muyskens, Dan Keating and Samuel Granados, "Mapping How the United States Generates its Electricity," *Washington Post*, March 28, 2017, washingtonpost.com/graphics/national/power-plants.

Labels, labels, labels—they're everywhere. At the supermarket, we find lists of ingredients and corresponding tables of sugar and salt, vitamins and minerals. Fast food restaurants now list calorie counts next to menu items. Why don't energy providers give you similar information? Not all energy sources are the same. Some sources come from our backyards; others transport energy thousands of miles. Shouldn't you, as a consumer of energy, know where that energy is coming from, and what process is creating that energy? In 2016, 34% of US power was generated from natural gas, 30% from coal, 20% from nuclear, 7% from hydro, 6% from wind, and 1.5% from solar and oil.[1] These percentages vary widely by region. Shouldn't you be able to decide the kind of energy you want to buy, just like you decide what kind of food you put in your body?

# 04



# Learn how to use the technology around you to gather information about your world and environment

It turns out a smartphone can be a
pretty sophisticated way to gather
data and information about the world
around you. You're probably already
using the camera, and you might even
know that the images you take are
tagged with the date, time, and your
GPS location (known as "metadata").
But your phone is gathering lots of
other interesting information at
the same time. It's measuring light
and sound levels, movement and
acceleration. Even the angle at which
you hold it is a data point. Some phones
even measure temperature, and most
can be connected to inexpensive sensor
devices that will turn a phone into a
portable environmental monitoring
laboratory. Let's dig deeper and
uncover the mystery of how energy
moves around.

# 05

ANDREA POLLI

# Learn to create a basic electric circuit, use a multi-meter, and read a circuit diagram

Now we're getting down to the
nitty gritty. When we talk about
understanding how energy systems
work, we're talking about basics.
How do you get energy from one place
to another? How does it transform
into something useful like light?
Understanding this is not often intuitive
to us because energy is invisible. At
worst, we see or smell the impacts of
energy production or consumption—
black smoke, or the smell of oil or
gas—but otherwise our senses don't
register very much. As human primates,
we understand the world through our
bodies; we want to touch things with
our hands, manipulating stuff in the
real world using our opposable thumbs.
Really understanding the basics of
what energy is made of means rolling
up your sleeves and twisting wires
together. This means not just thinking
outside the box, but literally opening
it up to see what's inside.

ANDREA POLLI

# 06

# Learn to write computer programs

After twisting wires and soldering,
you now have an embodied knowledge
of how things work; electronics have
ceased to be intimidating. You have felt
the materials, and you know that this
is something real, something physical.
Now, you're going virtual. You may not
build the computer you'll use to program
data (or maybe you will!), but you've
got a sense of what it would take.
Programming is the next step because
it's behind all the apps, websites,
and social media that you use. Take a
minute to think about all the choices
that other people make to create any
online experience for you, and the other
choices that they could have made.
Just like the layers of regulation that
have gotten us to a complex system of
energy production and consumption, our
information production and transmission
systems are layered with decisions
that were made decades ago. Are these
still the best choices? The only way to
answer that question is to learn what
the choices have been and what other
possibilities there may be.

# 07

# Learn how to harvest energy from the sun, the wind, the earth, and your body

ANDREA POLLI

You've hacked sensors, microcontrollers, laptops, and smartphones. You've moved energy around all these devices, but you still haven't connected what you are doing with the source of energy. Luckily, your devices probably don't need a lot of energy. You might charge up your smartphone as you bike to work. You might find (or even build) a small wind turbine or solar panel. You might make an energy-producing floor and have a dance party. The possibilities are endless; you can start small and soon become your own "nanogrid"— a one-person point of power and connectivity among multiple devices.

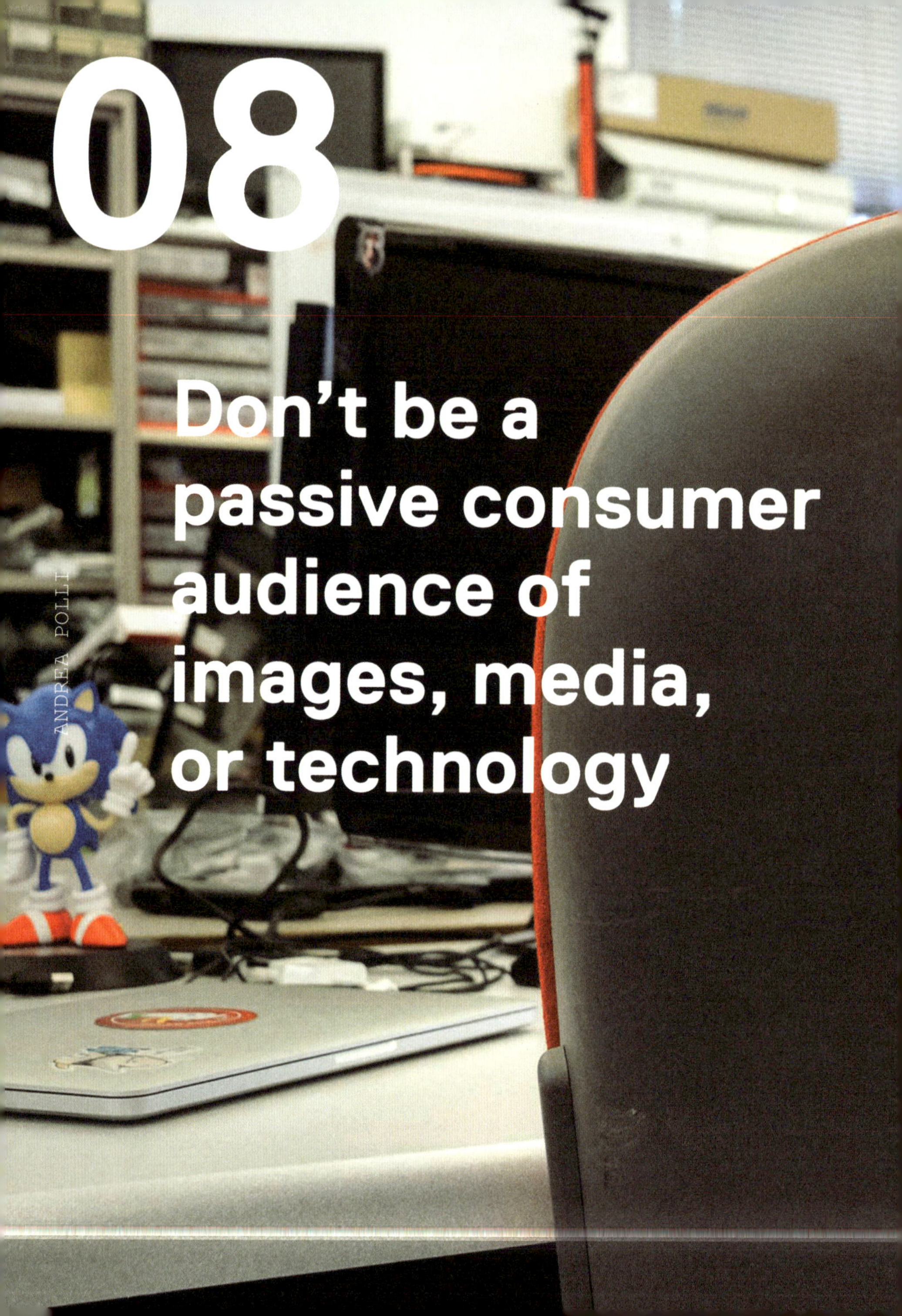

08
Don't be a passive consumer audience of images, media, or technology
ANDREA POLLI

Something has changed in you. You don't see the world from the same perspective. You've learned how to look at media and technology in a new way. By making images, programs, and even energy yourself, you understand more about how these are constructed or might be used to manipulate you. Those layers of complexity have been peeled back, and now you're more confident. You can look at a power line and know where that energy came from and where it's going. That latest tweet from a reality show star doesn't seem so important anymore. The political tweets do, though, especially the ones in your local community. You start to follow your state and local legislators, and suddenly that new proposed building code has a lot more meaning. You see the big picture, and you're getting involved.

# 09

Understand
that your life
is inextricably
intertwined with
your use of energy
in all forms

ANDREA POLLI

You are the crux of *Hack the Grid*. You are a part of everything you consume— food, material goods, and energy—and everything you consume affects the world you live in. It's like a giant feedback loop, and now you know you need those loops everywhere, even to write a useful computer program. The thing is, just like you decide what's looping in your code, you should be able to choose what you send around to that bigger feedback loop in the world. As we say in computing: "garbage in, garbage out." Know how to gather good data, understand what it means, and make your choices based on quality information that you have verified yourself, not junk that someone else feeds you. You are made of energy and have the power.

# 10

# Learn from what others have done, share your experiences, and build your own communities of grid-hackers

ANDREA POLLI

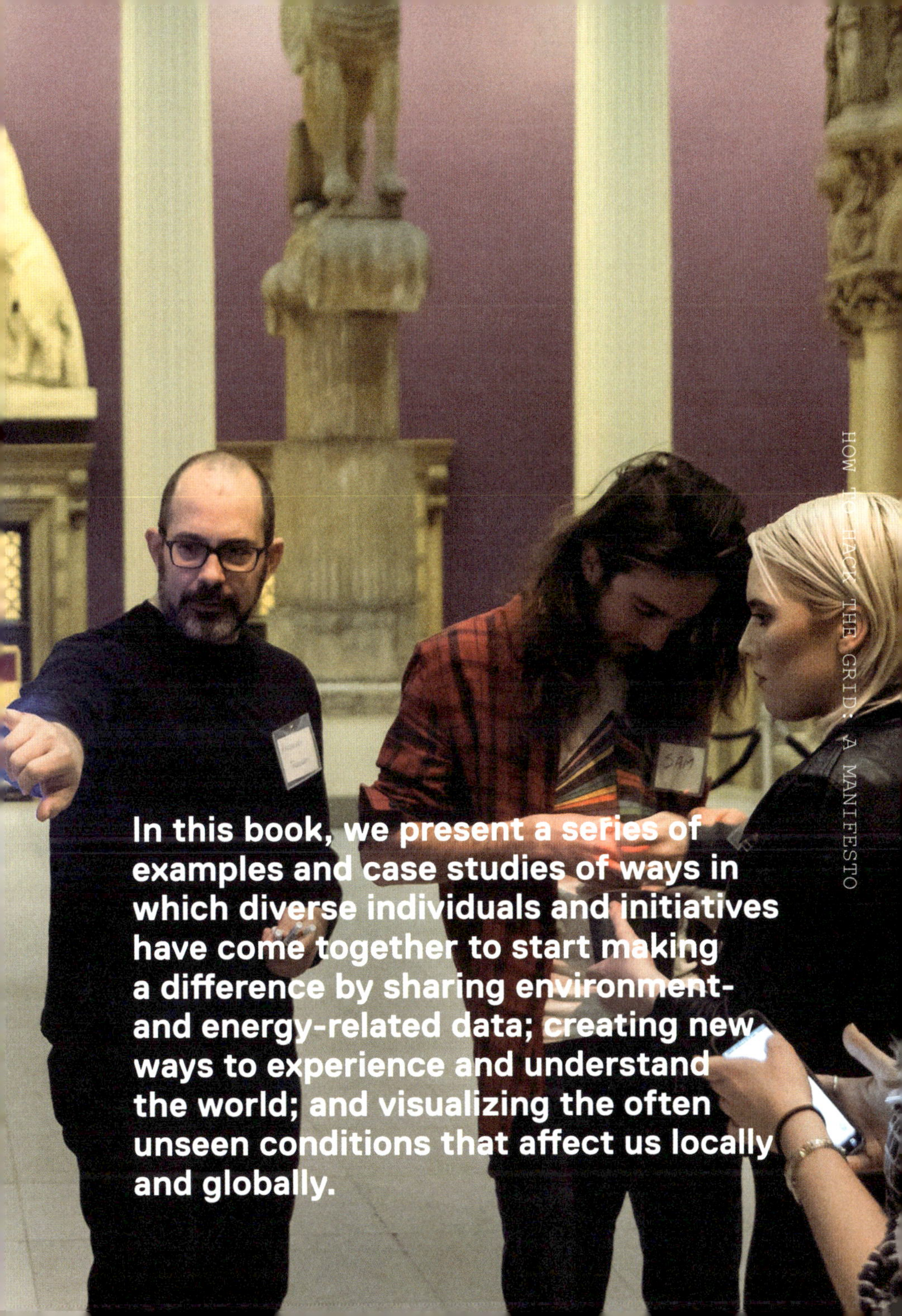
In this book, we present a series of
examples and case studies of ways in
which diverse individuals and initiatives
have come together to start making
a difference by sharing environment-
and energy-related data; creating new
ways to experience and understand
the world; and visualizing the often
unseen conditions that affect us locally
and globally.

THE

# HACK

# GRID

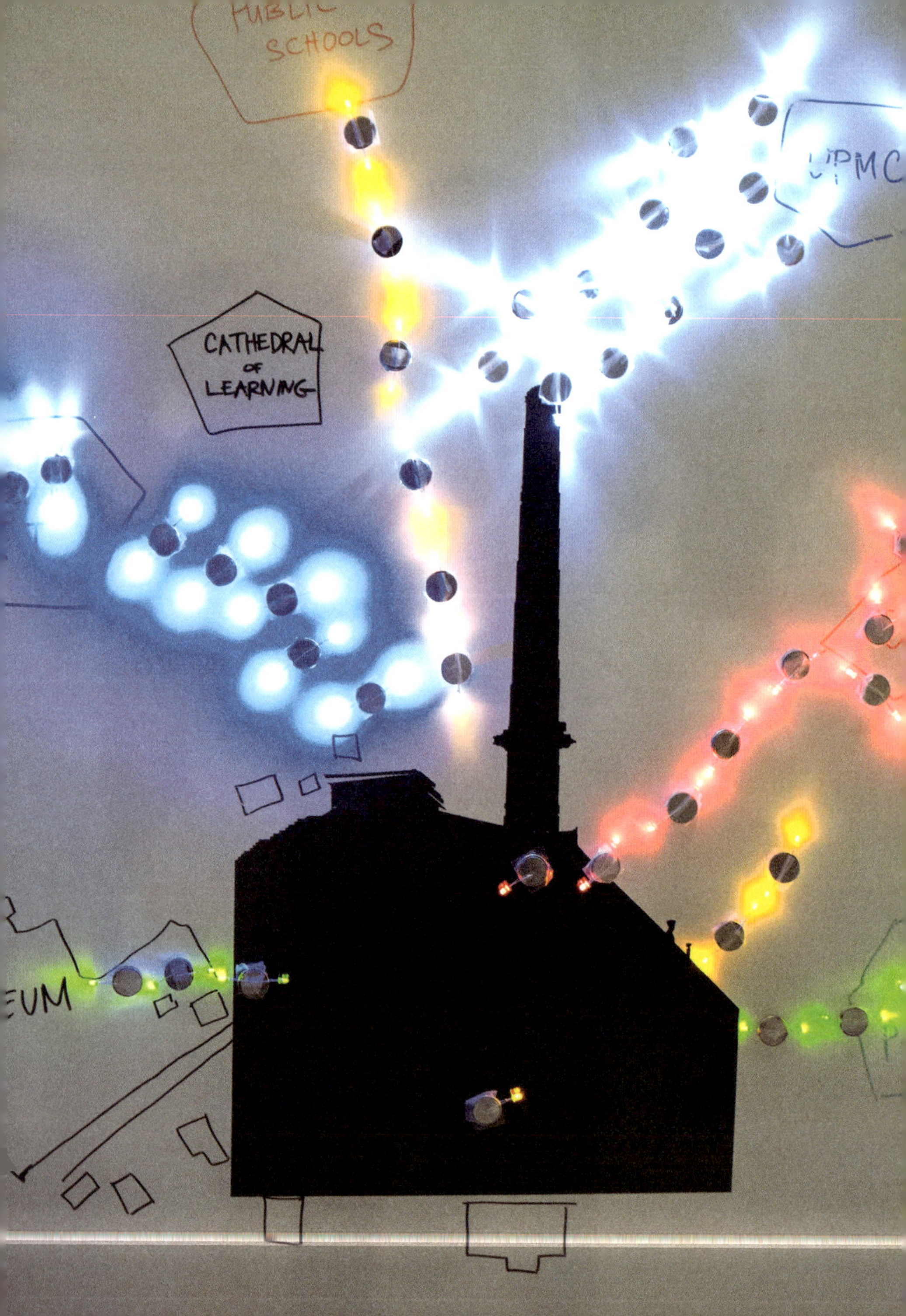

PUBLIC
SCHOOLS
UPMC
CATHEDRAL
OF
LEARNING
EUM

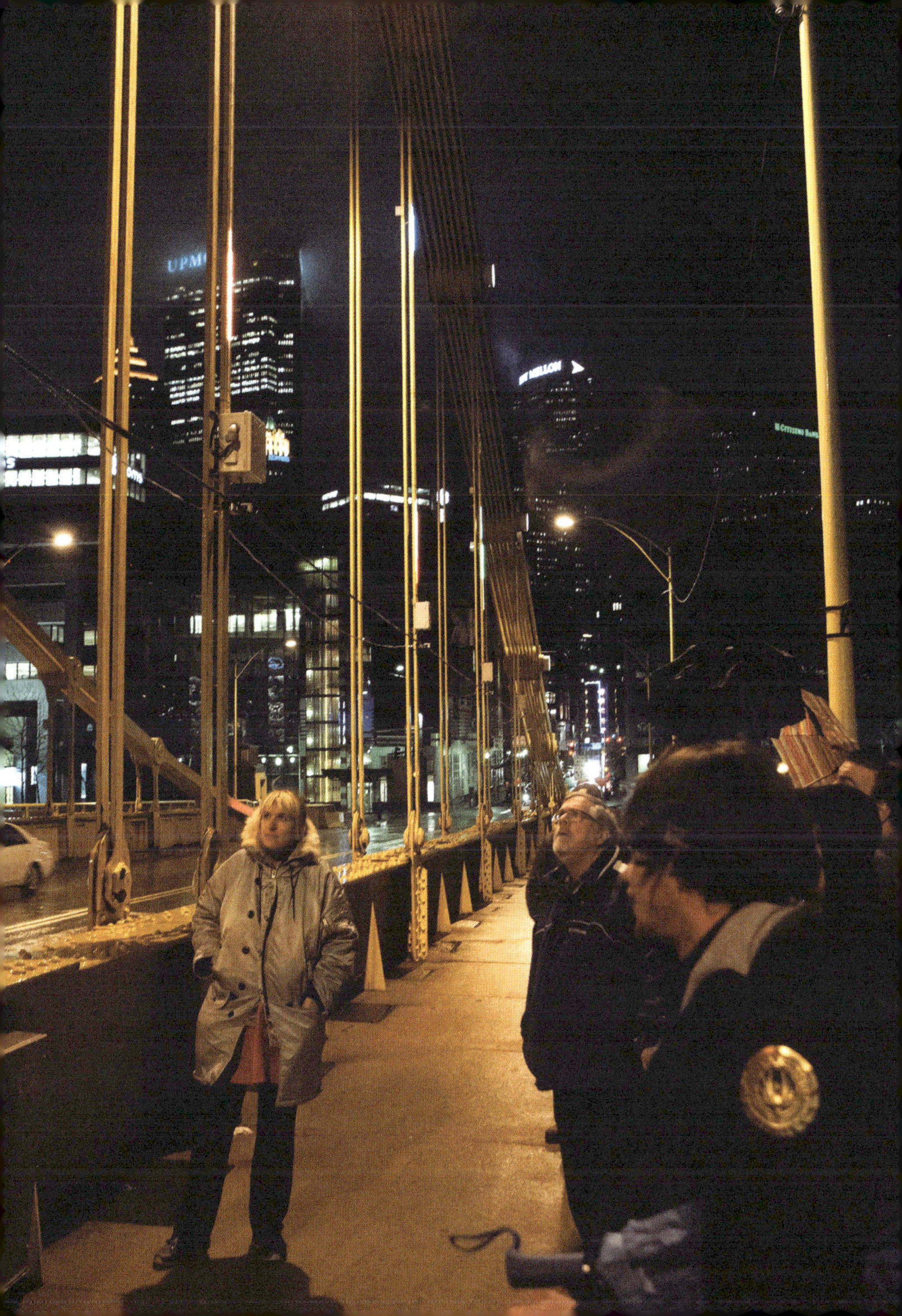

UPMC
BNY MELLON
Citizens Bank

# Contents

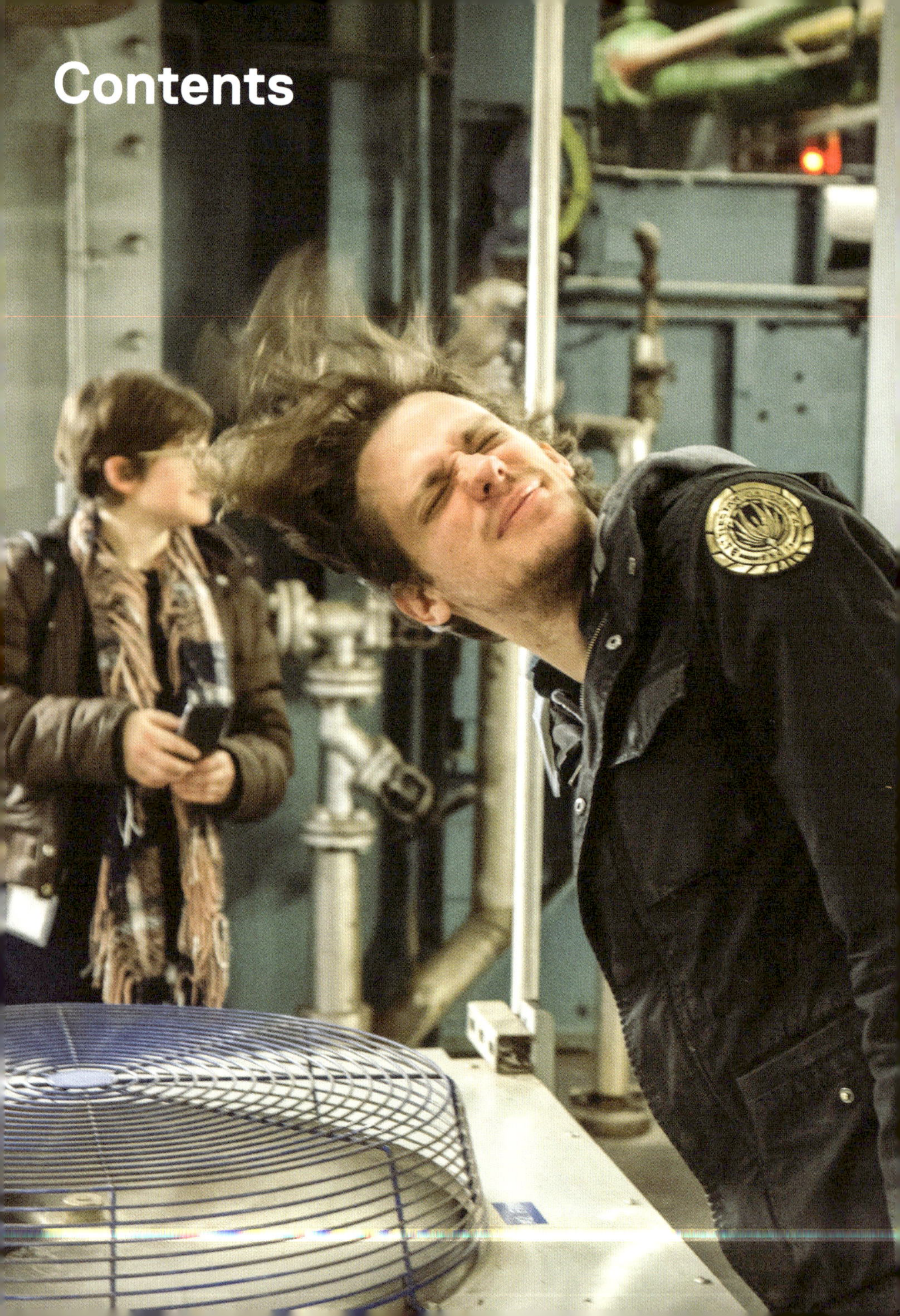

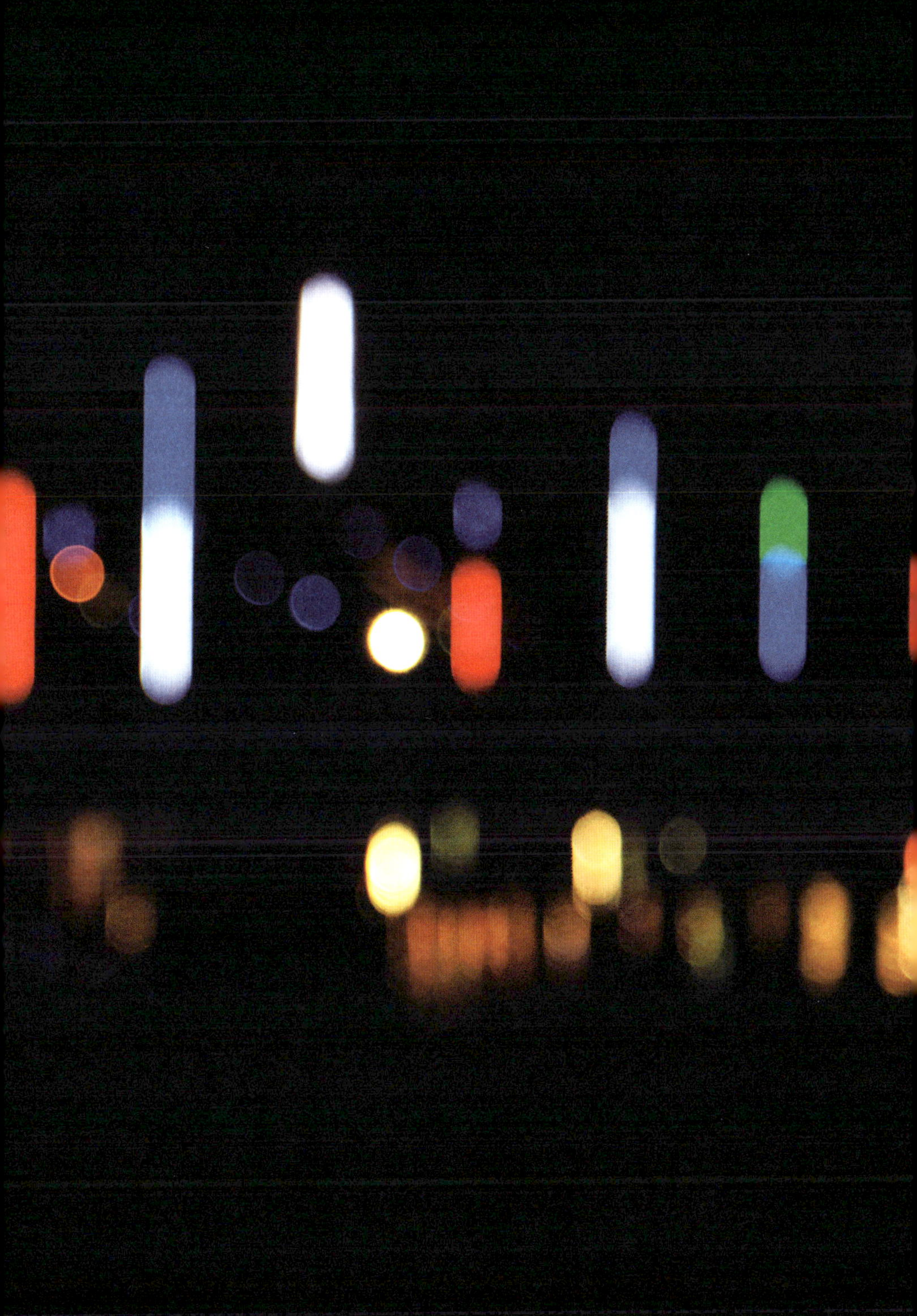

**The power of photography is not exclusive to the camera as we know it.** Conceptually, it goes far beyond the materiality of the instrument and the prints, proofs, and files that it produces. Photography has established a critical crossover between sight and action. The what, when, and how of picture-making assumes an almost moral imperative, asking "What do we need to see? What do we want to save?" Channeling the technical innovation of the camera without relying on its specific machinery, artist Andrea Polli harnesses the photographically inspired tools used in environmental data visualization. Her work invites us to look carefully at the world we inhabit, the energy we consume, and the information in which we are awash. When there is something that we cannot literally "see"—from particulate pollution to electrical power— she finds a way to make it an image, and motivates us to learn more about it.

As an incubator for innovative thinking on photography, the Hillman Photography Initiative at Carnegie Museum of Art is committed to expanding the definition and scope of the photographic image. Polli's project is one of four included in the Initiative's second cycle, LIGHTIME, which positions photography within the interdisciplinary discourses of light, time, and measurement. Guided by Divya Rao Heffley, Senior Program Manager for the Initiative, this cycle was developed in conjunction with a team of creative agents—Brooklyn-based artist Steffani Jemison; New York-based artist Liz Deschenes; Yale professor of Women's, Gender, and Sexuality Studies and American Studies Laura Wexler; and CMOA curator of photography Dan Leers. Their diverse perspectives were essential in considering the local and global issues to which photography responds.

For *Energy Flow*, launched in November 2016, Polli used over 27,000 multicolored LED lights along the vertical cables of the Rachel Carson Bridge to visualize wind speed and direction, all of which is also captured by a weather station on the bridge. In January 2017, she led "Hack the Grid with Artist Andrea Polli: Light, Energy, and Environmental Sensing—A Responsive Vision for Public Art," a series of CMOA workshops for the public that examined how we experience, analyze, and visualize environmental information, with smartphones and commercially available apps that can measure air and light as a starting point. In *Hack the Grid*, Polli documents these workshops, as well as past and current public art works.

This artist's book is the culmination of a project that began in 2014, when Polli presented *Particle Falls* on the facade of the Benedum Center in Pittsburgh. The large-scale digital installation projected real-time animations that tracked particulate pollution within the immediate vicinity, creating a cascade of visual stimuli that was at once a riveting aesthetic experience and an alarming reminder of the need for cleaner air.

Andrea Polli makes environmental crises and atmospheric data visible, and encourages us to combat invisibility through investigation. This is what she calls "hacking"—exploring and exposing the utility of everyday technologies. With equal attention to physical devices and artistic interventions, *Hack the Grid* aims to inspire and unleash creative responses to the things that we see—and don't see—around us. At CMOA, we are proud to present Polli's work to you.

**Lynn Zelevansky**
The Henry J. Heinz II Director
Carnegie Museum of Art

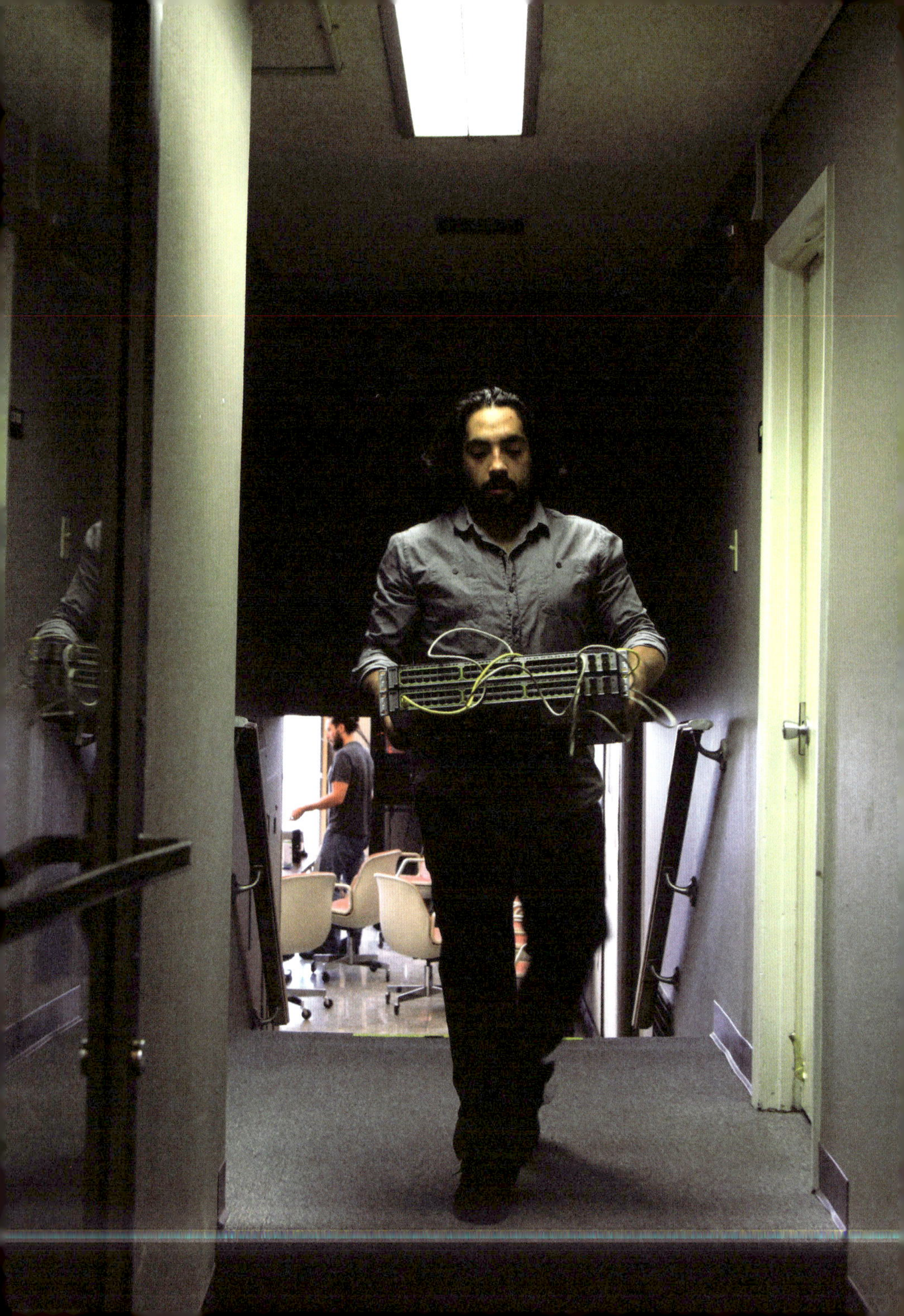

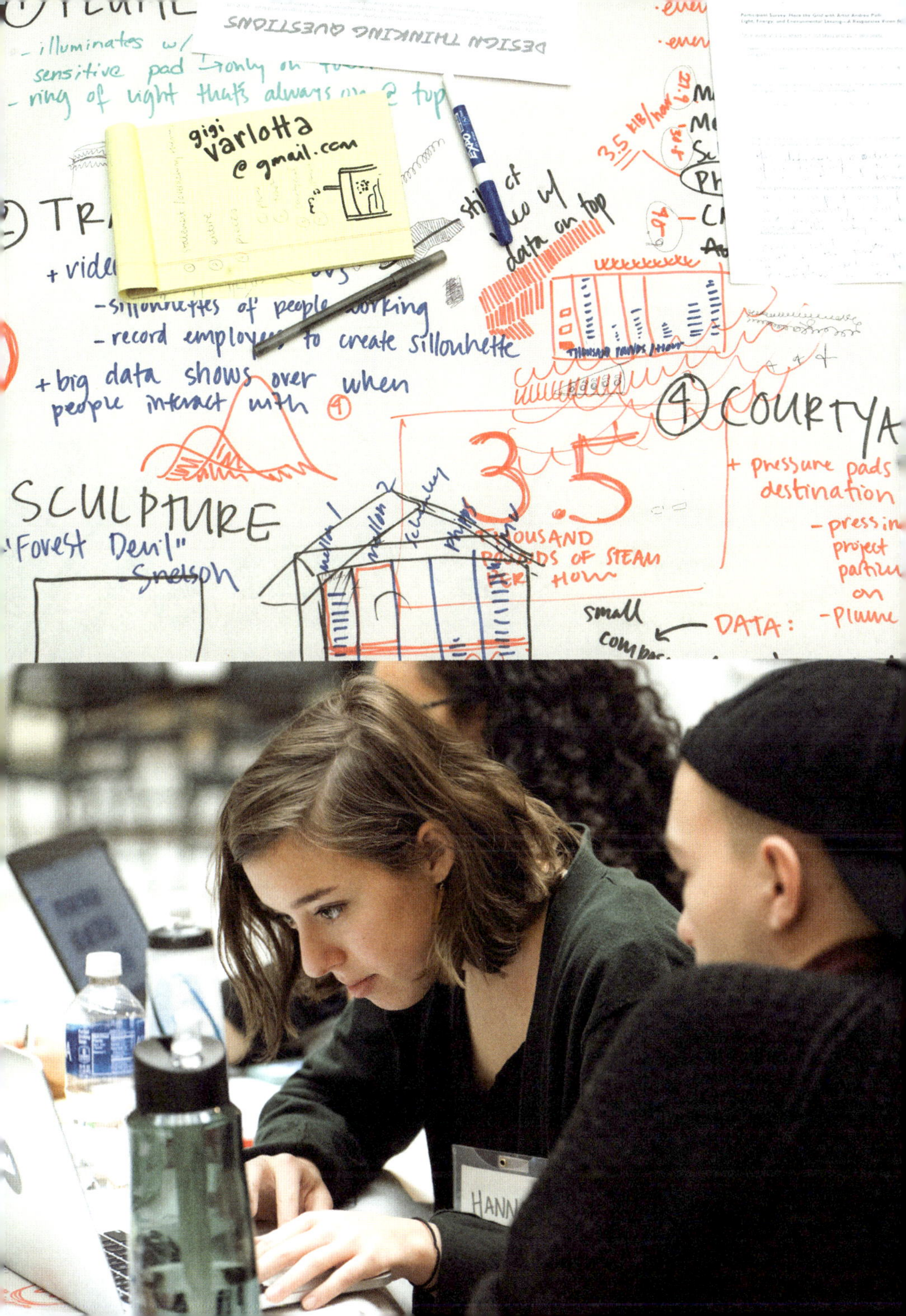
PLUME
- illuminates w/
sensitive pad if only on
- ring of light that's always on @ top
DESIGN THINKING QUESTIONS
gigi varlotta @ gmail.com
② TRA
+ vide
- sillouettes of people working
- record employees to create sillouhette
+ big data shows over when
people interact with ④
SCULPTURE
"Forest Devil"
- Snelson
3.5
THOUSAND POUNDS OF STEAM PER HOUR
small combus.
DATA:
④ COURTYA
+ pressure pads
destination
- pressin
project
particu
on
- Plume
strip of
video w/
data on top
3.5 THOUSAND POUNDS / HOUR
HANN

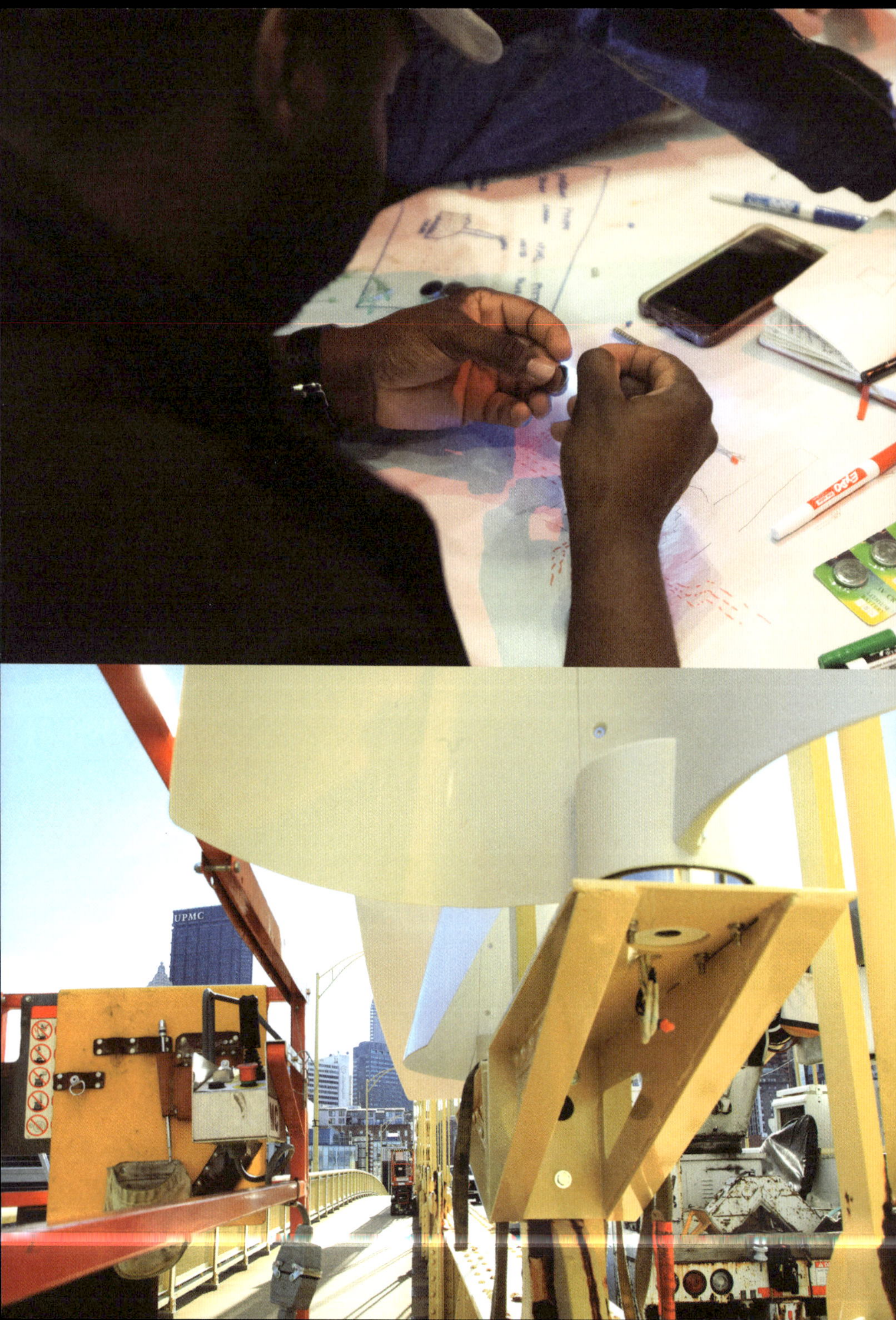

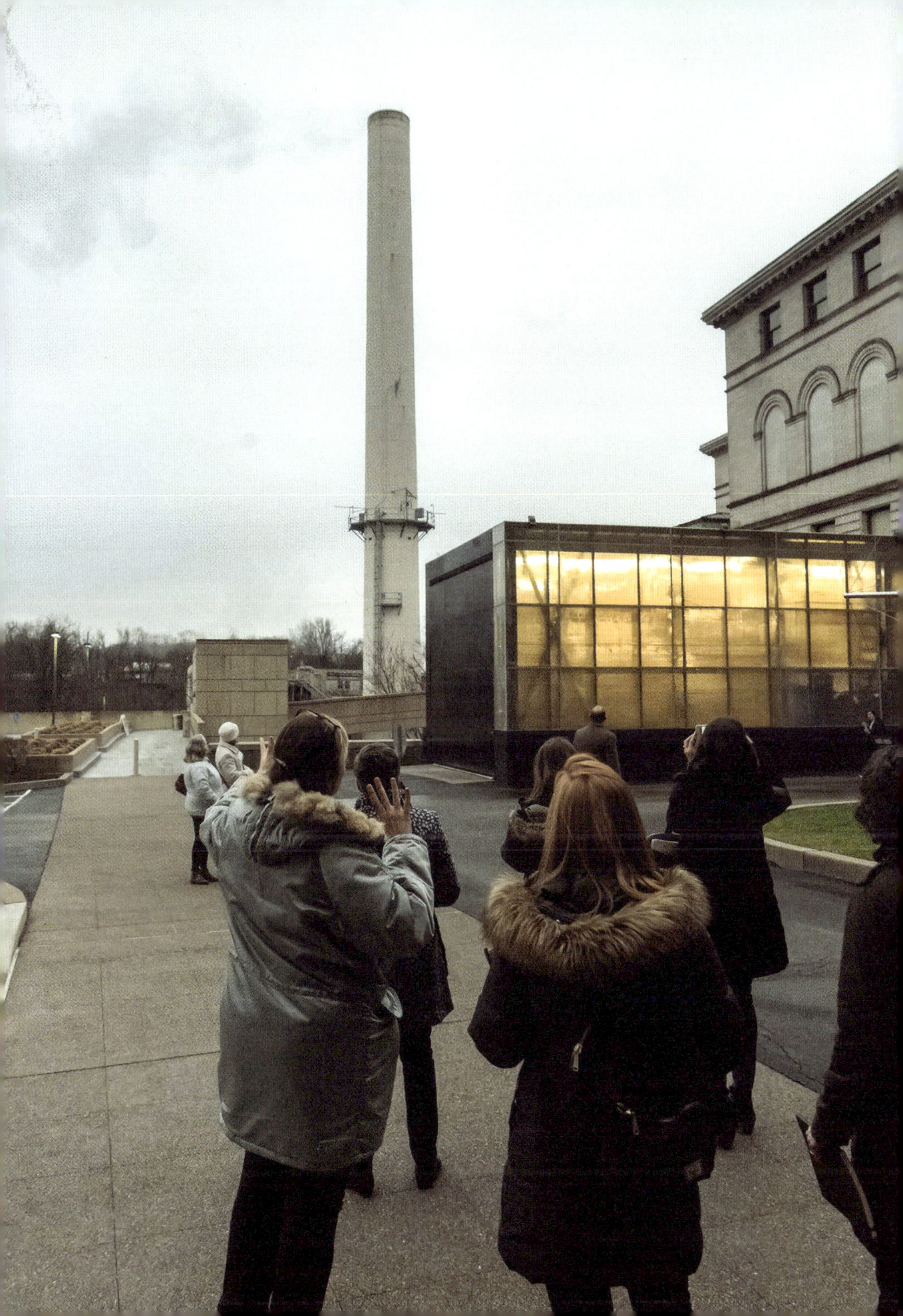

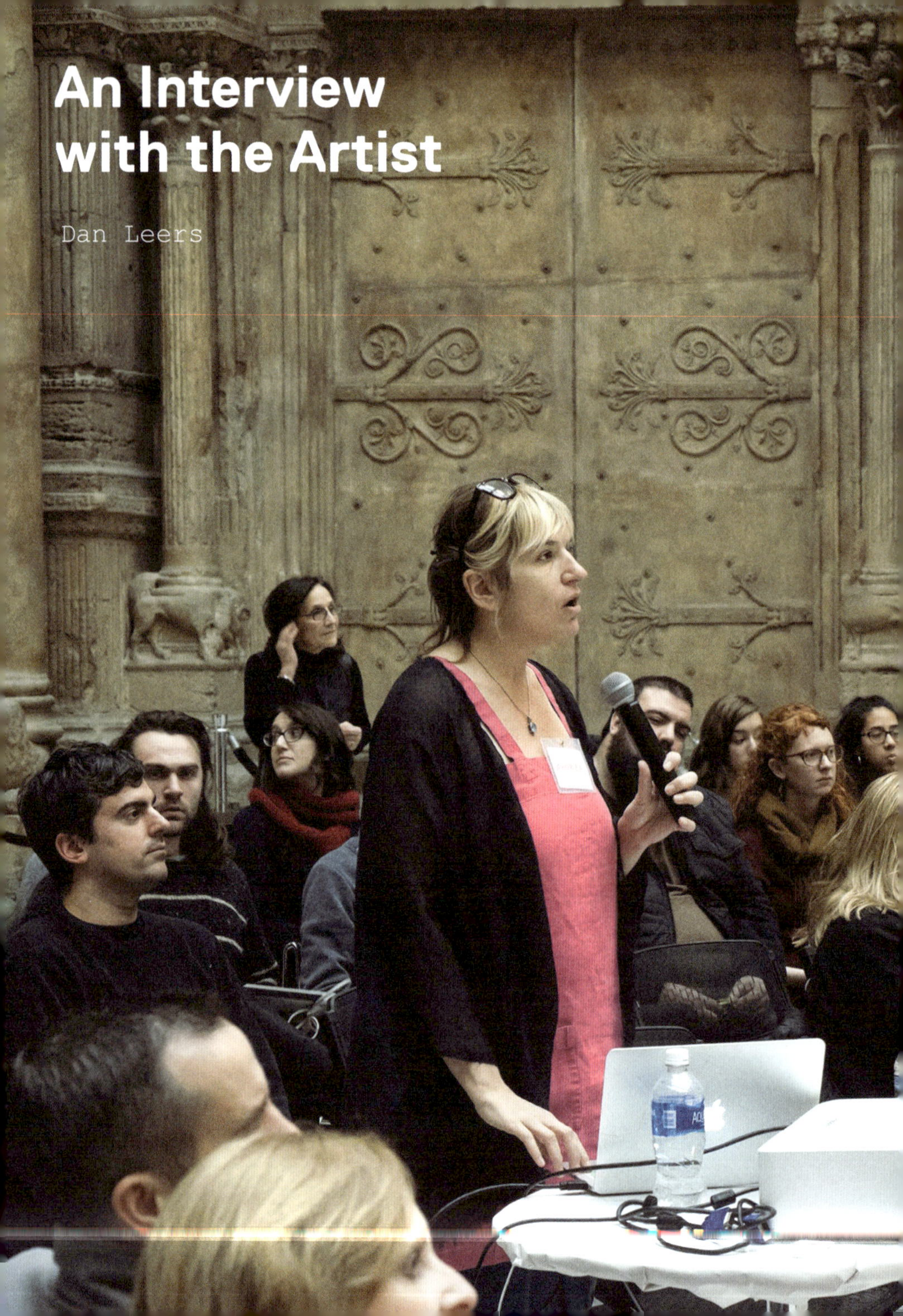

# An Interview
# with the Artist

Dan Leers

For the second cycle of the Hillman Photography Initiative, Carnegie Museum of Art invited artists to investigate contemporary social issues through photography's measurement of light and time. Andrea Polli's project addressed the relationship between light and environmental sustainability using data visualization. Here, she engages in a dialogue with CMOA curator of photography Dan Leers about the role of photography in her practice and its ability to change people's perceptions and behaviors.

*Dan Leers*

*Can you can talk about your first formative experience
with a camera?*

Andrea Polli

I think the most significant moment for me was a
convergence of photographic technology and digital
technology. I saw my connection to photography with
the scanner, the digital camera, and using code directly
to create naturalistic forms. I often think about the
origin of the term "photography" as "drawing with
light." For example, when chaos theory was popularized
in the late 1980s, I was doing a lot of coding to create
images that you could zoom into infinitely, or which
looked like naturalistic forms.

*Dan Leers*

*I wonder if you can talk a little more specifically about that
practice of scanning. What was your process, and what were
you thinking about as you were scanning these forms?*

Andrea Polli

When I was using a film camera, I would be frustrated
by the grain. I would try to zoom in and zoom in and
zoom in, not unlike a kind of fractal image, and would
eventually get the grain, or even worse, pixelation—a
very regularized form of pixels. But I could scan a leaf
or a feather or a piece of grass and really zoom in on it
like a microscope.

*Dan Leers*

*I love that idea of zooming in, and in a way, it seems like
that's a big part of your practice. You identify a set of data
points and zoom in to think about what they mean, both
in an isolated fashion and potentially as part of a larger*

*constellation. A loosely related question is whether you think photographically. In your mind's eye, are you "drawing with light" as you're zooming in on these data points?*

Andrea Polli

That idea is important to at least one aspect of how I work and how I think. I've done a lot of work with sound and the sonification of scientific data. I remember when I was teaching a class in sound design at the School of the Art Institute of Chicago, and another faculty member told me that he felt it was important that students learn reel-to-reel tape because you could see what was happening—that it made the sound more visible and tangible.

I remember looking at the tape and saying, "Yeah, but you can't see the waveform." For me, it's really important, when using sound, that you can see the sound wave and you can zoom in or out to see the shapes and the form. That, to me, is really seeing the sound.

*Dan Leers*

*You mentioned your issues with film and its inherent graininess. We're now living in the digital age. How can you explain, or account for, the power of a digital image specifically to effect change in a way that film cannot?*

Andrea Polli

One of the sea changes of digital imagery versus celluloid is the use of the metadata. Beyond the zeroes and ones that make up digital images, there's a whole host of other information that gets attached to them, and then that gives us the ability to catalogue them, organize them. It gives us more background information about those images: where that image was taken, what kind of camera was being used, what time and date. All that kind of information, to me, has been a sea change, a transformative point, in terms of the convergence of digital media.



*Dan Leers*

*What's the appeal to us as viewers of an image? Do we think in images or in photographs more so than we think in, say, numbers? Does that impact how we behave as viewers?*

Andrea Polli

I think it depends on the person and the time in their life. There have been times when I've thought much more in sound than images. But at the same time, if I'm thinking about numbers, then I'm also likely thinking about a visual representation of those numbers.

If you imagine all the metadata that's out there in the world—in all the selfies and everything else—it's completely overwhelming. So how do you turn that into some sort of visual form? It makes me think about, for example, one of the early representations of the internet as a constellation.

I've worked a lot with meteorologists and atmospheric scientists, and one meteorologist told me that the work of atmospheric science today would not exist without visualizations. There's just no possible way that work can be done without visual representations and satellite images. Otherwise, it's just impossible for a scientist to understand what's happening.

*Dan Leers*

*It seems to me, though, that there is a fundamental difference between your data visualizations and, to stick with that weather metaphor, the Doppler radar pictures we see on the nightly news. That's a visualization of weather and*

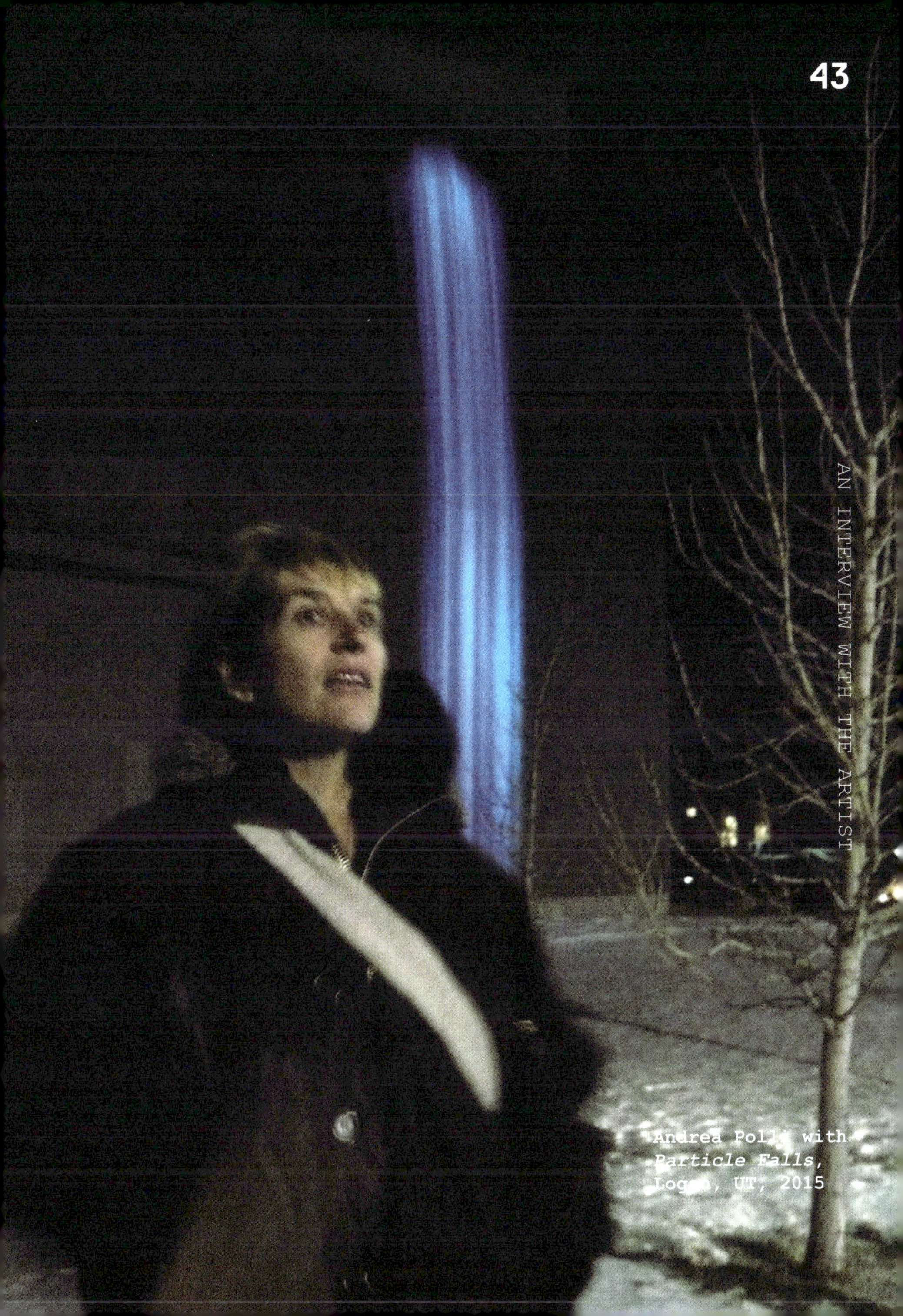

Andrea Polli with *Particle Falls*, Logan, UT; 2015

*atmospheric data being compiled for one context, but you're working in an entirely different context. Where does that separation happen for you? How is what you do different than what a weatherperson or a meteorologist does?*

Andrea Polli

When I was corresponding with that meteorologist and he was trying to communicate something about what was happening in the weather, he'd say, "Okay, I'm going to send you these visualizations that I've been generating, and I want you to give me a critique." He was asking for an almost art-like critique, because he wanted to know what was being communicated by his abstraction of the data.

There is a lot of blurring between disciplines that's happening now, and that can be a good thing. I don't think that we in the art world have served ourselves that well by staying siloed. Right now, at this particular moment in history, we're in danger of losing the NEA [National Endowment for the Arts] and, well, I think that as an art community, we haven't made enough of a compelling argument about why what we do is important to society.

*Dan Leers*

*I find it interesting that the meteorologist was essentially asking about the effectiveness of an image to evince some sort of emotional reaction on your part. There's this idea of art, and specifically photography, as a form of activism. For you, what are some of the effective strategies that you can use in an image to change a person's behavior, or change public policy and understanding in the political sphere?*

Andrea Polli

Imagery can be incredibly compelling. Recently, social scientists have written about the "red globe" as an important example—this is a visualization of global warming that shows the entire globe in red. In a way, you just don't need any other information there.

For me, that's been my strategy: using real-time data so that people are seeing things as they change. A truck pulls up while they're looking at *Particle Falls*, and the work transforms into a fireball; you can see the impact of burning fossil fuels right there.

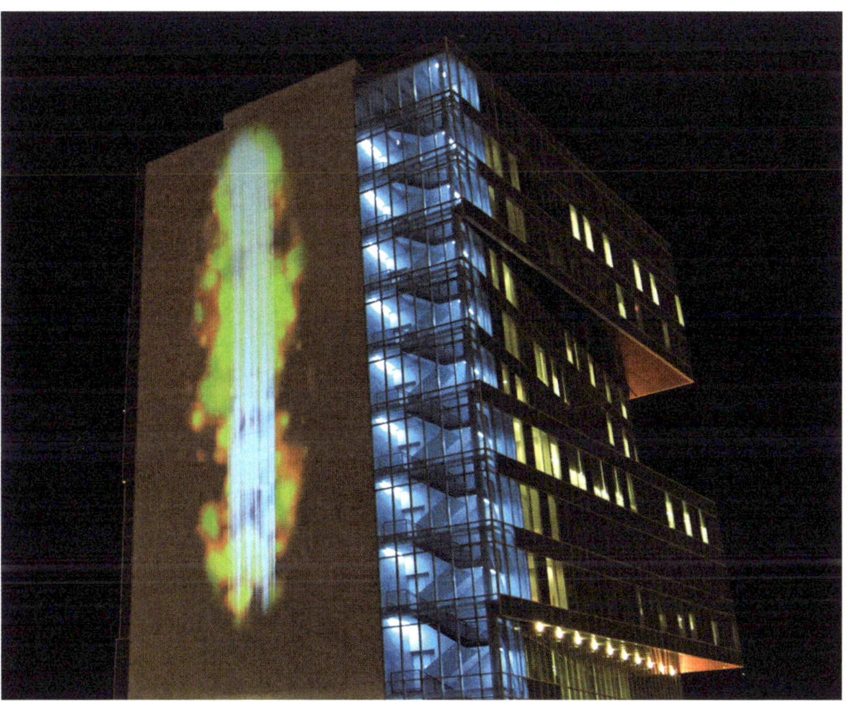

*Particle Falls*, Charlotte, NC, 2016

Think of Al Gore's graph in *An Inconvenient Truth* (2006). It's not necessarily a rich image, but the idea that the graph is going off the screen, and he's up on the crane trying to draw it—that's another kind of symbolic representation.

My new colleague here in Art & Ecology at the University of New Mexico (UNM) is Subhankar Banerjee, and his images of some of the wildlife impacted at the Arctic National Wildlife Reserve have made a compelling case for saving that reserve. You could probably make an argument that the imagery has been one of the central things that has had political impact, or that can have political impact.

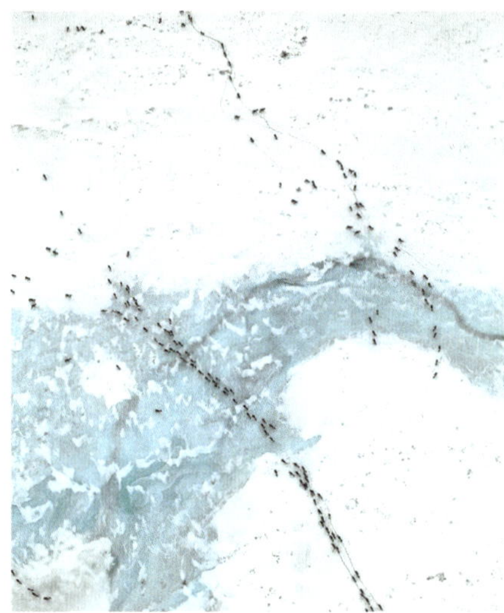

Subhankar Banerjee, *Caribou Migration I*, from the series "Oil and the Caribou," photograph, 2002

### Dan Leers

*You've mentioned the environment and climate change several times, and you also mentioned* Particle Falls. *When you started out with this project, did you already have the idea to do a waterfall visualization and were you looking for data to fit that? Or was it the other way around?*

### Andrea Polli

I had been doing interviews with scientists who were working on air quality, and I learned about some new sensors that were able to detect a very fine particulate pollution of PM2.5, which is 2.5 micron. A grain of salt is about 80 micron, so 2.5 is very, very small—easily lodged in the heart or the lungs. One of the scientists was working in Colorado, and she told me about the famous brown cloud that sometimes floats over Denver. People had these wonderful homes with beautiful mountain views, but at the time, for a large percentage of the year, the mountain view would not be visible because of that cloud. People became engaged with air quality activism there; for one thing, the brown cloud was reducing property values. When I heard that, I became interested in imagery in relation to air quality. Because very often, you can't see bad air. In big cities, tall buildings don't offer the same mountain vistas that you get out in Colorado. I thought, "How could I do something that would allow you to see pollution in an urban setting?"



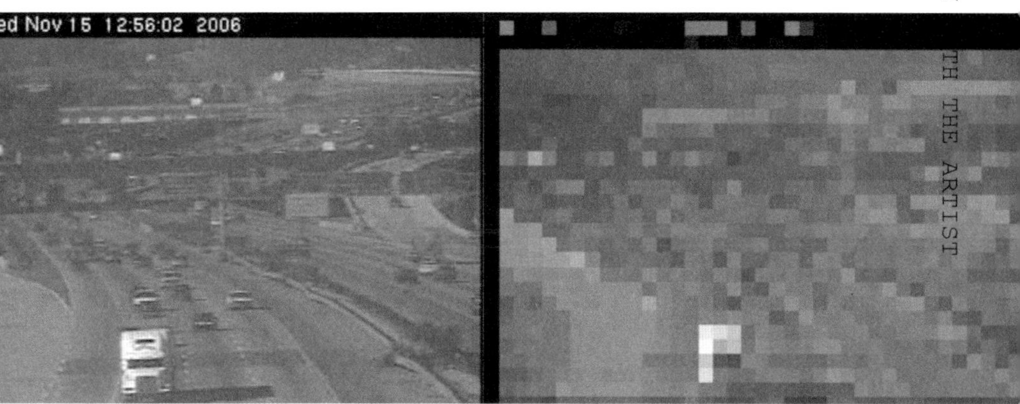


Andrea Polli, from *Airlight*, 2007

I did a piece before *Particle Falls* that was called *Airlight*. "Airlight" is a phenomenon in which the interaction between particles in the air and sunlight causes a bright light to blur your distance vision. I used imagery from a real-time traffic cam that I pixelated based on how much particulate pollution was in the air, as well as other pollution. I used all kinds of data on air quality that the EPA was collecting in different places.

I created *Airlight* for a few different locations, and that was the precursor to doing *Particle Falls*. The idea of the waterfall emerged as part of the public art project I did for San Jose, California. The goal, in part, was to emphasize the positive environmental impacts of a new light rail system that they were building. They wanted a projection on the AT&T Building, which is very monolithic. There are no windows. When I stood there and looked at this really tall building, I thought, "Oh, it's like a cliff. What if a forgotten corner of the city was turned into a jungle scene, and the AT&T Building became something like Victoria Falls?"

*Dan Leers*
*When you were invited to recreate that project here in Pittsburgh, in 2014, did you already have an idea of what Pittsburgh looked like, or what kind of city it is, and did that impact your decision to agree to do this?*

Andrea Polli

I don't think I really did. I knew about Carnegie Mellon University, and that Pittsburgh had had a renaissance with technology after a history of industry. I knew about the focus on education and learning there.

What I found, though, was a community integrated with the sciences. For example, at the launch of *Particle Falls* there was a great group of people who came from the community and were concerned about air quality. There was one woman whose child was experiencing asthma attacks at school, and she wanted to get more air-quality sensors in the schools to understand why.

Some people were politically active or advocates, and some were scientists or engineers from the university. That's one thing I continue to find in Pittsburgh all the time: this mix of people from different backgrounds, and a freedom to work between those disciplines.





_Dan Leers_
_I want to ask one more set of questions that address your practice now. In particular, what role does photography play, and how has the rapid transition to digital continued to change it? Through smartphones and other consumer technology, anybody can start doing data visualization. I wonder how you are also using and harnessing these new tools._

Andrea Polli
Big question! My practice is really integrated with my teaching and running my lab. I have an interdisciplinary lab at UNM called The Social Media Workgroup. We approach imagery and image making in a number of different ways, from digital video that we've got out on our YouTube channel to imagery that we are getting from microscopes. We're doing a lot of bio art and design work. I just finished a National Science Foundation project with some collaborators at the Center for High Technology Materials, where they're doing nanotechnology, nanomaterials, and so we interact with images even down to the nanoscale.

It's interesting because there's also a lo-res thing that's happening that I really like and enjoy. We used LED strips on the bridge for _Energy Flow_, and we have a couple of different projects here in New Mexico that are also using the LED strips as a platform. I was just talking to a student who programmed real-time animations for these strips based on weather data, and he said it was a

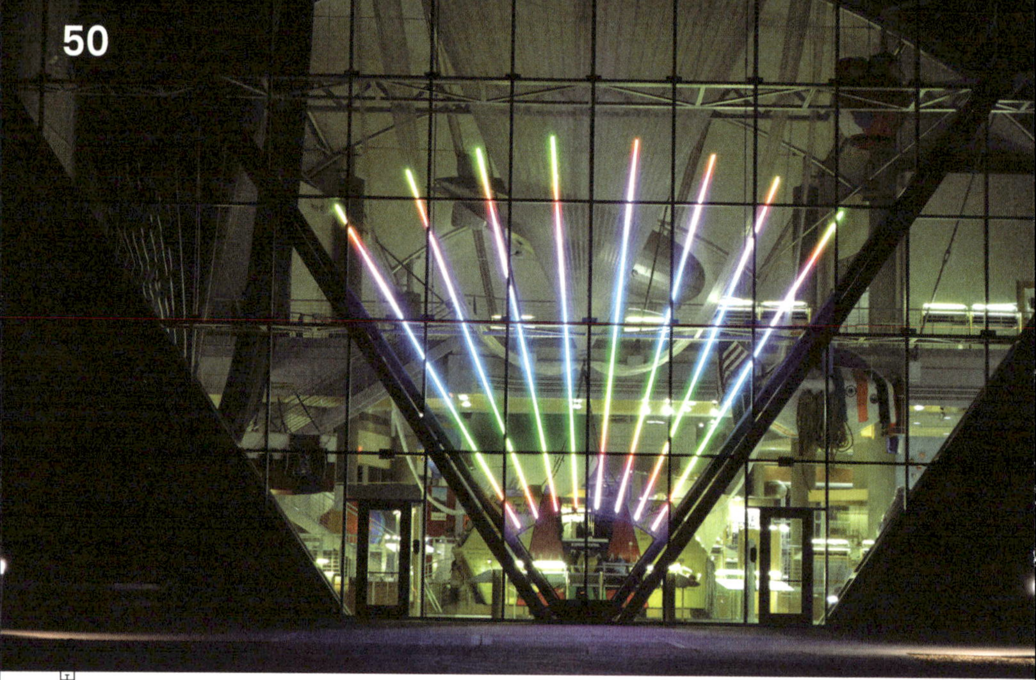

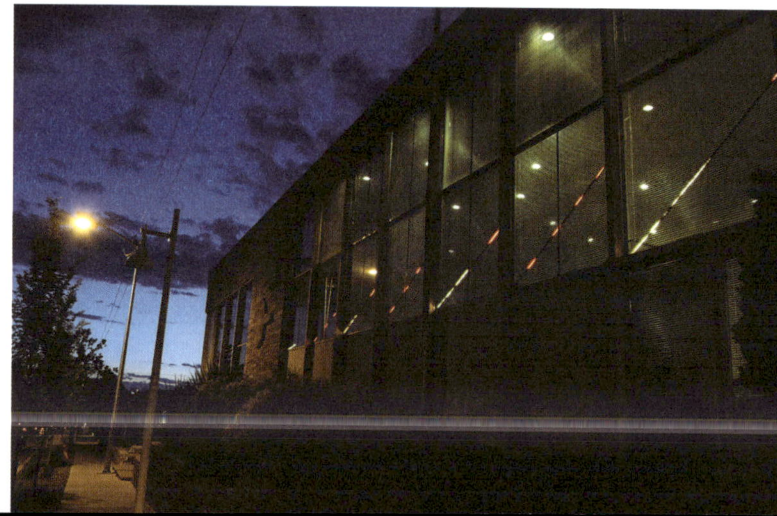



Above: *Skylight*, created with student researchers from Polli's Lab, The Social Media Workgroup, at the Anderson-Abruzzo Balloon Museum, Albuquerque, NM, 2014

Below: *Data Central*, created with student researchers from Polli's Lab, The Social Media Workgroup, at the Center for Advanced Research Computing, Albuquerque, NM, 2017

challenge to use such a low-resolution platform. Maybe there's a level of reduction, or an abstraction, that's helping us resolve all of this big data. Perhaps that's a strategy right now.

*Dan Leers*
*In a way, it's almost the exact opposite of when you started, where you wanted such high resolution that you could go as deep as possible, and now it sounds like you might be advocating for something else.*

Andrea Polli
It's a multi-pronged process. We're still looking in microscopes and making images and trying to understand things on that level, but we're also creating imagery for communication on public platforms. So that reduction and abstraction can be helpful in making information… well, if not more clear, then at least more noticeable. The lower resolution highlights the movement. For my public works, the shape and the character of the movement communicates the data more than the detail of the image.

*Dan Leers*
*There's a bit of democratization happening there too, right? You don't need the highest-quality optics to do this stuff. What advice do you give to your students and others in terms of using the camera sensor and the data sensors on their smartphones? How do you encourage them to think creatively that way?*

Andrea Polli
Everything is becoming so much less expensive and more accessible. There are low-cost attachments for your camera, or for your phone, that will measure

particulate pollution now. Your smartphone has a suite of sensors. You've got a tilt sensor, an accelerometer, a light sensor, a microphone sound sensor. You can use those. You've got GPS.

We've created *DataGather* in my lab, which is an app that gathers all the data that is being generated by these sensors and puts it into an accessible database. There are other platforms out there that will also allow you to do that. All of this is a part of image or media literacy in my view.

Image or media literacy is being able to understand what it is you're seeing. For example, I think about some of the images and videos of police brutality that have been in the news, and how they're seen and interpreted in context or out of context. We're all carrying around cameras and image-distributing machines in our pockets, and although we think we understand these images, I'm not sure that we really do. I would like to see more of a focus on image and media literacy in terms of really understanding the meaning, for example, of a documentary image.

### Dan Leers

*Are there strategies that you pursue in teaching this to your students?*

### Andrea Polli

If you are taking images and editing them in different ways to create different messages, that gives you a hands-on understanding of what's possible. Being someone who manipulates images to tell different stories based on a different order or edit or selection can really teach you a lot.

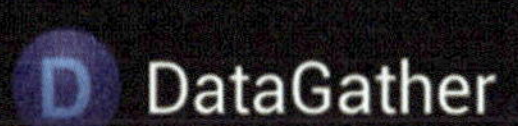





Smartphone screenshot from *DataGather*, created with student researchers from Polli's Lab, The Social Media Workgroup

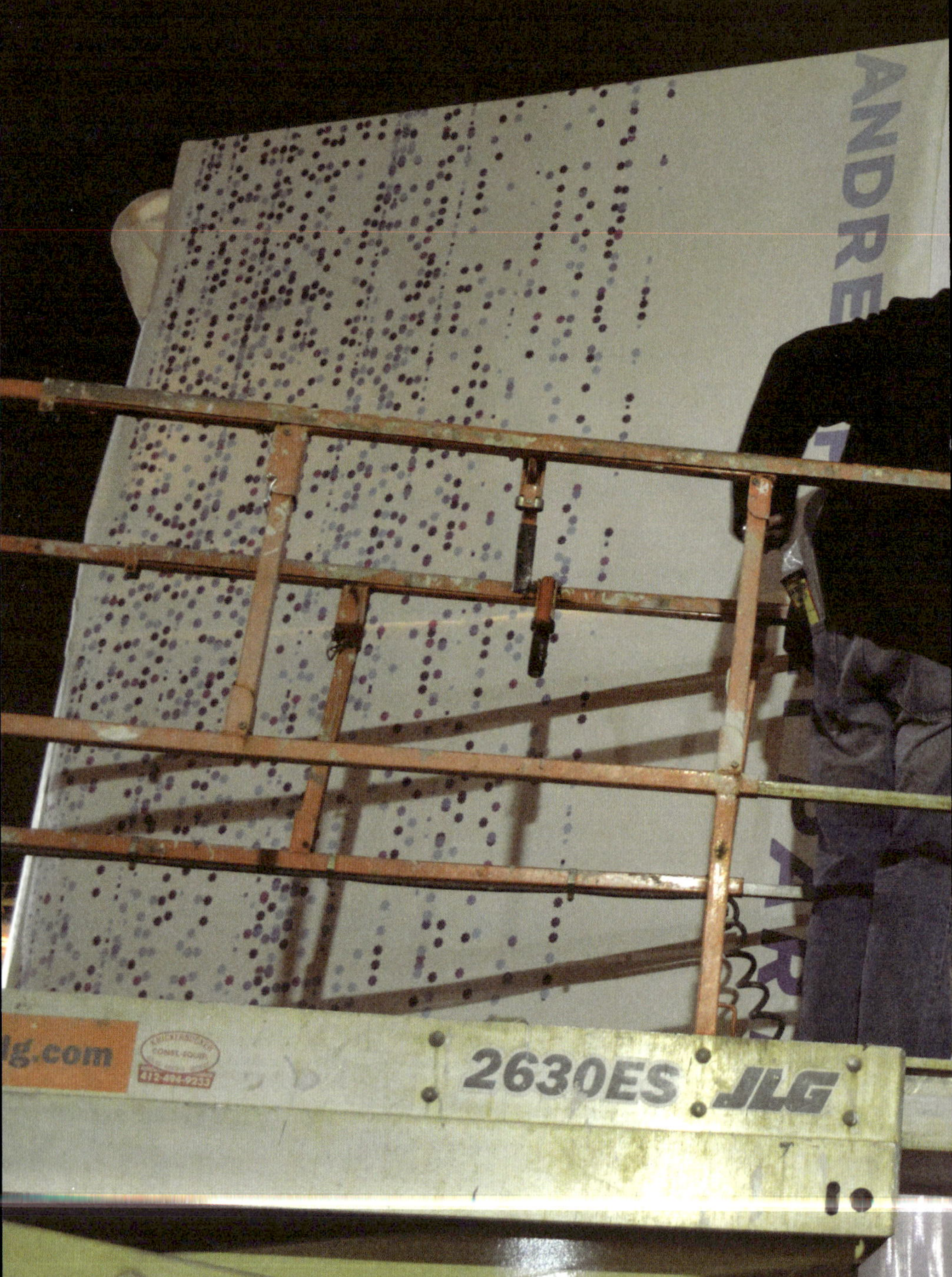
ANDRE
lg.com
2630ES JLG

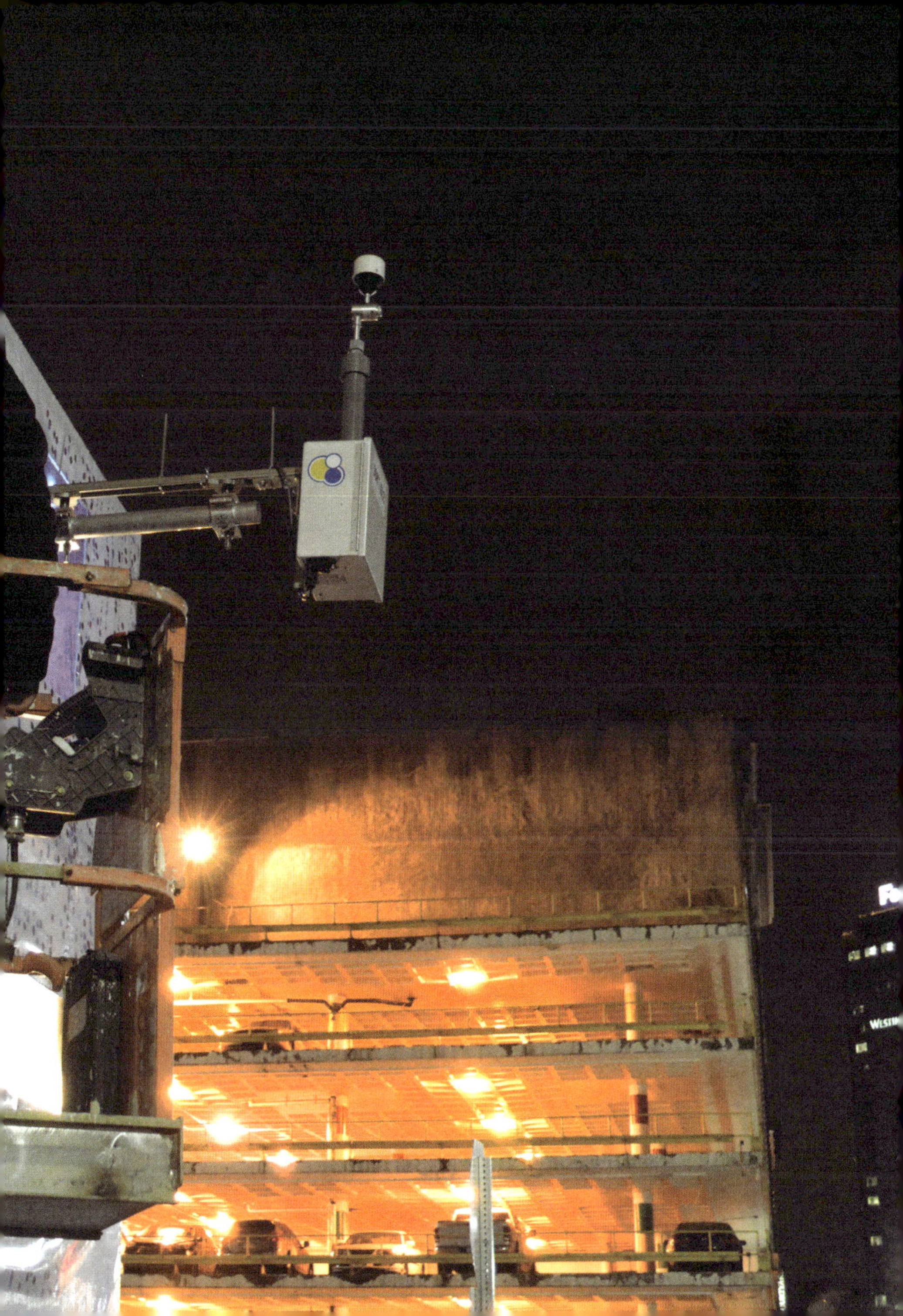

# Why Particles?
# Why Pittsburgh?
# Why *Particle Falls*?

Philip R. S. Johnson

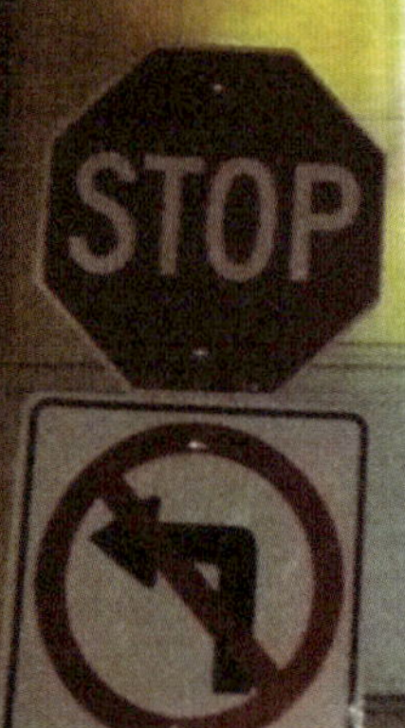



Particle Falls,
Pittsburgh, PA,
2014

In November 2014, Andrea Polli installed *Particle Falls* at a busy downtown location in Pittsburgh. For this ingenious installation, an air monitor mounted next to the street transferred pollution data within seconds of real time into a cascading "falls" of blue light that illuminated the nearby facade of the Benedum Center for the Performing Arts. By projecting the city's air pollution as spots of fiery, flowing light on the wall of a major downtown landmark, Polli transformed a seemingly invisible problem into one that was impossible to ignore. Those viewing the falls from the street were now seeing the air pollution that they took in with each breath.

PHILIP R. S. JOHNSON

The installation was brought to Pittsburgh by The Heinz Endowments's Breathe Project with the support of the Office of Public Art and Flyspace Productions. The piece was intended to engage the city in a conversation about air quality—not only addressing the challenges, but also imagining ways to work together toward solutions. The Endowments launched the Breathe Project in 2011 in response to general civic disbelief and denial that air pollution was a public health and quality-of-life problem. Rigorous scientific evidence has shown that the city's air is unhealthier and dirtier than most urban areas in the nation. But many in Pittsburgh say, "Well, you should have seen what it was like thirty years ago!" Because of its history of heavy industry and current industrial footprint, Pittsburgh has a uniquely cavalier attitude about environmental health compared to many US cities.

Confronted with this social challenge, the Endowments set out to develop a platform to share information, generate innovative data visualization and stories, and weave together the work of constituencies that include community groups, academic organizations, environmental and health advocates, and medical professionals. While Pittsburgh's air has been steadily improving, the Breathe Project maintains that better is not good enough. Cities that thrive—attracting families and developing sustainable economies—know that their future and quality of life depend on having clean and healthy air. Our objective has been to find the right messengers to communicate the importance of clean air, thereby building awareness and activism that will engage the public to demand solutions that improve air quality. Artists such as Andrea Polli are central to this agenda.

Soot, or fine particulate matter, is comprised of liquid droplets and solid particles of varying chemical composition. These particles can be emitted from combustion activities such as industrial smokestacks, wood burning, forest fires, and restaurant charbroiling, as well as mobile sources such as cars, trucks, buses, construction equipment, trains, and barges. Particles

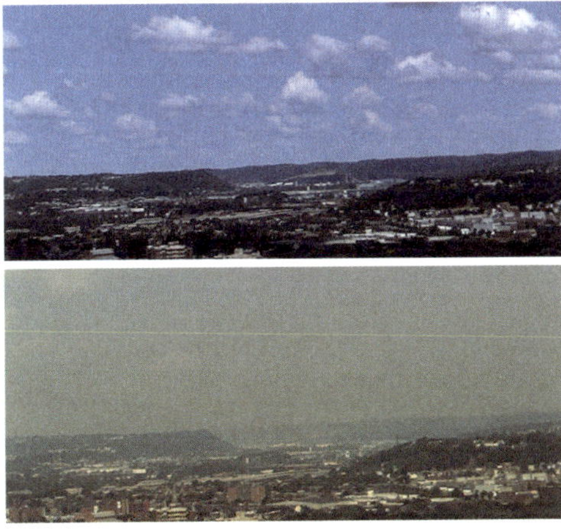

Views of the Pittsburgh skyline with variable air qualities

are also formed from the reaction of gaseous chemicals in the atmosphere after their emission from power plants, industrial facilities, and other sources.

Fine particles threaten the health of humans in every stage of life, from the cradle to the grave. Studies across the country have shown that prenatal, infant, and child exposures to air pollutants are associated with outcomes including premature birth and low birth weight; impairment of brain development leading to cognitive and behavioral disorders; and acute and chronic respiratory illness and disease. Particulate pollution also contributes to asthma, sends many thousands with respiratory and heart disease to hospitals and emergency rooms, and results in substantial lost school and work days. Fine particles also prematurely kill nearly 88,000 Americans each year, contributing to deaths from ischemic heart disease, stroke, lung cancer, and COPD.[1] Because there is no safe level or threshold of exposure to fine particles, death and disease occur even at pollution levels that are legal. This is not a trivial public health problem.

## *Pittsburgh*

In many ways, Pittsburgh is a preeminently livable city. Because of its cultural offerings, revitalized riverfronts, and manageable cost of living, it often refers to itself as "Most Livable." And yet Pittsburgh is also one of the most contaminated cities in the country. Among state and federal air quality measurement sites from nearly 300 urban areas, Pittsburgh ranks in the dirtiest 12 percent of monitored cities for fine particulate matter.[2]

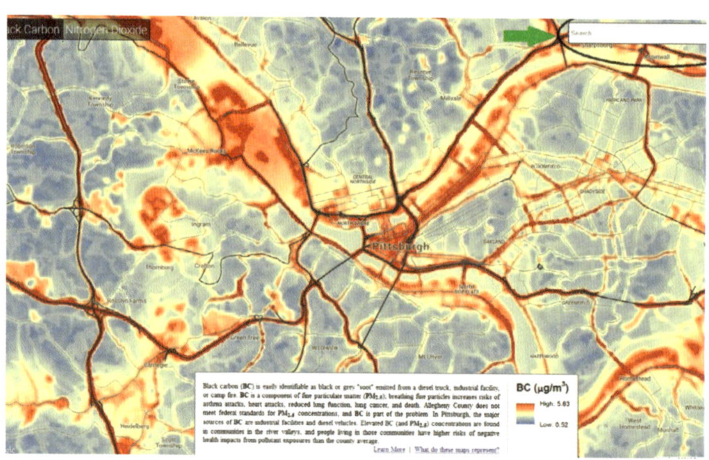


A map of black carbon air pollution levels in the Pittsburgh area

In Allegheny County, cancer risk attributable to industrial air pollution ranks in the highest 0.03 percent of all counties in the United States, according to the US Environmental Protection Agency's National

Air Toxics Assessment.[3] In 2016, the Pittsburgh metropolitan region had 249 days of air quality that could not be defined as "good," according to the Air Quality Index of the Environmental Protection Agency.[4] Allegheny County is among only a handful of the thousands of counties in the country that still fail to meet federal air quality standards.[5]

In Pittsburgh and Allegheny County, the major source of direct particulate matter is industry. Metallurgical coke production, steel manufacturing, coal combustion, and other sources of pollution comprise almost 60 percent of fine particles found in our air on average. Other large sources include cars, trucks, buses, trains, barges, and construction equipment, as well as residential wood burning. Across western Pennsylvania, another significant source of particles comes from coal-fired power plants. Scientists at Carnegie Mellon University have recently mapped Pittsburgh's air pollution: the city's river valleys are among the most polluted areas, especially where industry is concentrated or highways are situated.[6]

*Particle Falls*

While statistics present a grim picture of a pervasive public health menace, air pollution is actually a solvable problem. Some cities are showing they are up to the challenge. Studies have demonstrated that the EPA's clean air programs lead to large and measurable public health benefits that exceed implementation costs by a factor of more than thirty-to-one.[7] For every dollar spent to reduce air pollution, many more dollars are saved by avoiding thousands of heart attacks, millions of cases of respiratory problems, and millions of lost work or school days.

This is why, across the country, many public health leaders and civic officials have offered strong support for clean air as a high priority in the cities where they live. They have taken definitive steps to reduce pollution; they have aggressively championed clean air.

Thanks in part to growing public awareness, more Pittsburghers are also demanding clean air. A recent Allegheny County health indicator survey found that air pollution is the number one concern of residents. People want clean air, and they now understand that our government and politicians need to do more. We can't expect the public to see the value in changing light bulbs and other small-scale interventions when most of our pollution problem comes from heavy industry. And so the Breathe Project is challenged daily to demonstrate the pathway to cleaner air to our region's business, civic, and community leaders.

Spurring leaders to action requires more than articulating the numbers, science, and proven policies. We need innovative and creative work that can make information relevant and engaging to all. We need work that foments action and imperative. We need to continue to engage and support our creative doers—those who apply their talents and passions to the quest for clean and healthy air. Notable examples in Pittsburgh include engineers at the CREATE Lab, who democratize data through their low-cost Speck sensor, Breathe Cam monitoring system, and Smell Pittsburgh app; the photographers who organized the *In the Air: Visualizing What We Breathe* exhibition; and the community activists who devised the "Closed Window Award" and turned Millville into a hub of air quality community engagement. And, of course, Andrea Polli's *Particle Falls*.

Thanks to these and similar efforts, new allies have joined the effort to clean Pittsburgh's dirty air.

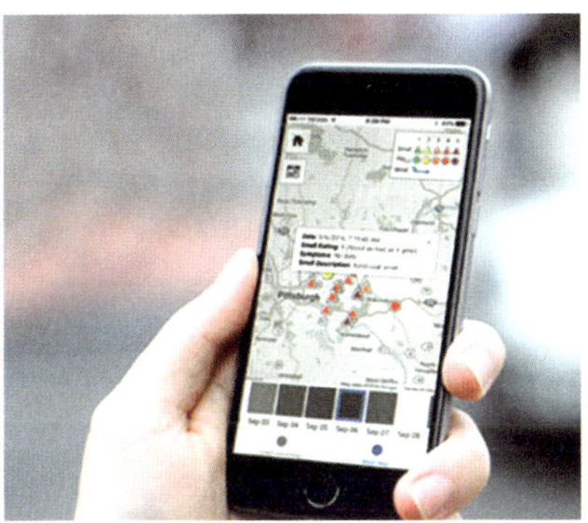

Interface of the Smell Pittsburgh mobile app, which encourages residents to report and track odors related to air quality in the region

More people now understand how air affects their own lives and their bottom line. Advocates for schools and children, parks and trails, outdoor enthusiasts, green and healthy buildings and homes, workplace sustainability, and neighborhood revitalization and development are taking an active role. So, too, has the health care and medical community become more engaged in understanding and addressing the impacts of air pollution on children and the elderly.

While forces of the status quo remain, our civic conversation has changed. Pittsburgh is starting to experience a transformation toward a more equitable, just, and sustainable city. Individuals, communities, and neighborhoods—especially those experiencing disproportionate harm from environmental challenges—are demanding more accountability of their political leaders. More people are taking steps to reduce their contributions to poor air quality and, at the same time, are demanding a faster response from regulators to hold large pollution sources accountable. But we are far from done as long as our city's air remains among the dirtiest in the nation.

It has become clear to many that if Pittsburgh truly wants to compete with other cities socially, culturally, and economically, then it must move from the ranks of the worst air quality in the nation to the ranks of the best. Until then, Pittsburgh cannot claim the mantle of a truly livable city. To do so is hypocritical.

In the spirit of swifter transformation, here are three things that our creative leaders can do to help ensure that political and regulatory leaders do their part to clean up Pittsburgh's dirty and unhealthy skies:

_1._ Build alliances, generate socially oriented ideas, and support the needs of communities to foster human well-being.

_2._ Develop and execute material that integrates personal or community-based experiences while working directly with impacted individuals and community members.

_3._ Translate the evidence to make it relevant, sharable, and applicable to all.

Notes

[1] Aaron J. Cohen, Michael Brauer, Richard Burnett, et al., "Estimates and 25-year trends of the global burden of disease attributable to ambient air pollution: an analysis of data from the Global Burden of Diseases Study 2015," *The Lancet* 389, no. 10082 (May 2017): table 2, accessed July 31, 2017, thelancet.com/journals/lancet/article/PIIS0140-6736(17)30505-6/fulltext#sec1.

[2] This percentile rank was determined from average annual particle pollution out of 317 urban areas in the US using EPA data from 2013 to 2015. Breathe Project, accessed July 31, 2017, breatheproject.org/learn/breathe-meter.

[3] United States Environmental Protection Agency, National Air Toxics Assessment, accessed July 31, 2017, epa.gov/national-air-toxics-assessment.

[4] United States Environmental Protection Agency, Outdoor Air Quality Data, accessed July 31, 2017, epa.gov/outdoor-air-quality-data/air-data-aqi-plot.

[5] United States Environmental Protection Agency, Nonattainment Areas for Criteria Pollutants (Green Book), accessed July 31, 2017, epa.gov/green-book/green-book-pm-25-2012-area-information.

[6] The Breathe Project, accessed July 31, 2017, breatheproject.org/learn/pollution-maps.

[7] United States Environmental Protection Agency, Clean Air Act Overview: Clean Air and the Economy, accessed July 31, 2017, epa.gov/clean-air-act-overview/clean-air-act-and-economy.

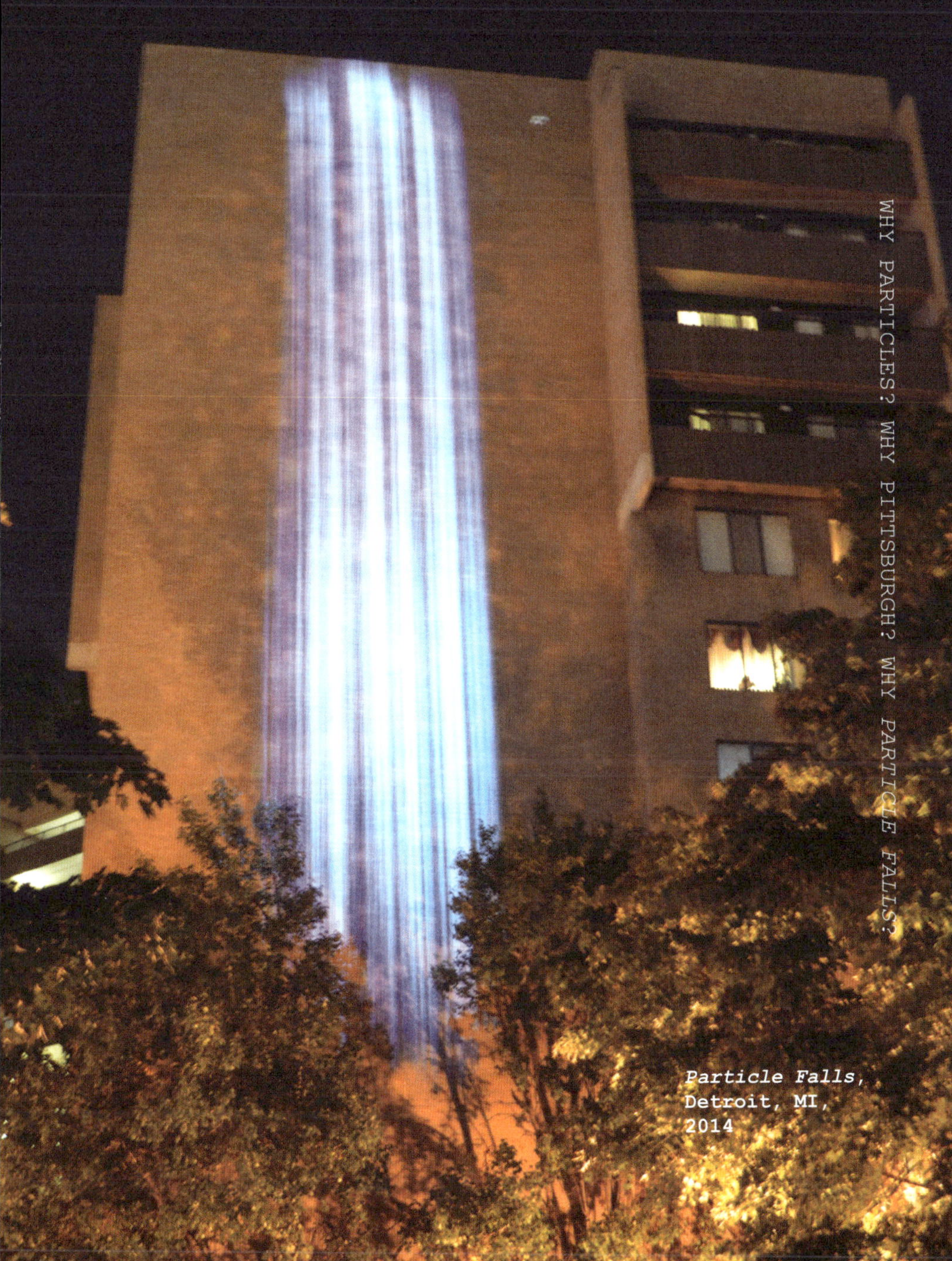

WHY PARTICLES? WHY PITTSBURGH? WHY PARTICLE FALLS?
Particle Falls,
Detroit, MI,
2014

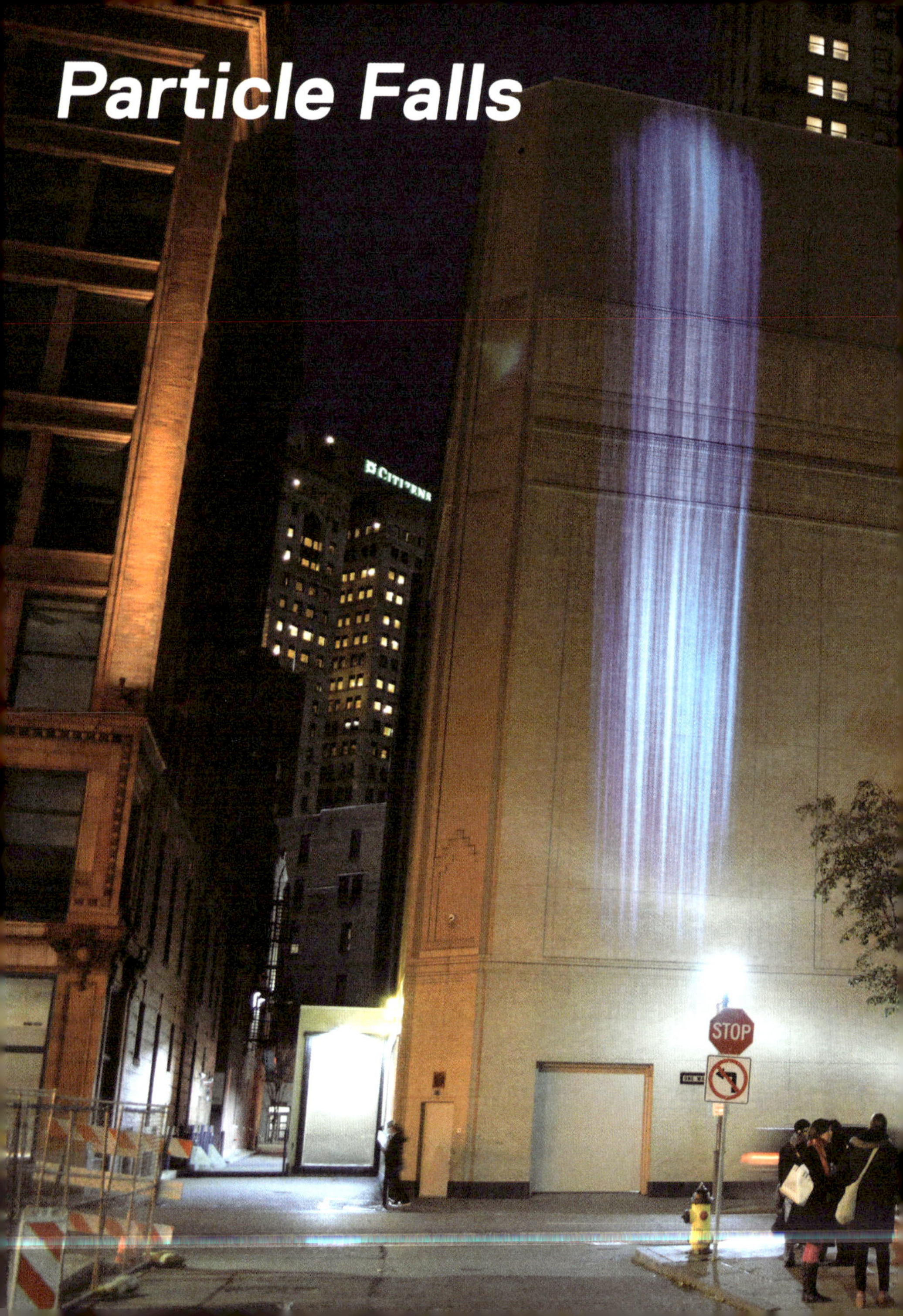
Particle Falls
CITIZENS
STOP
ONE WAY

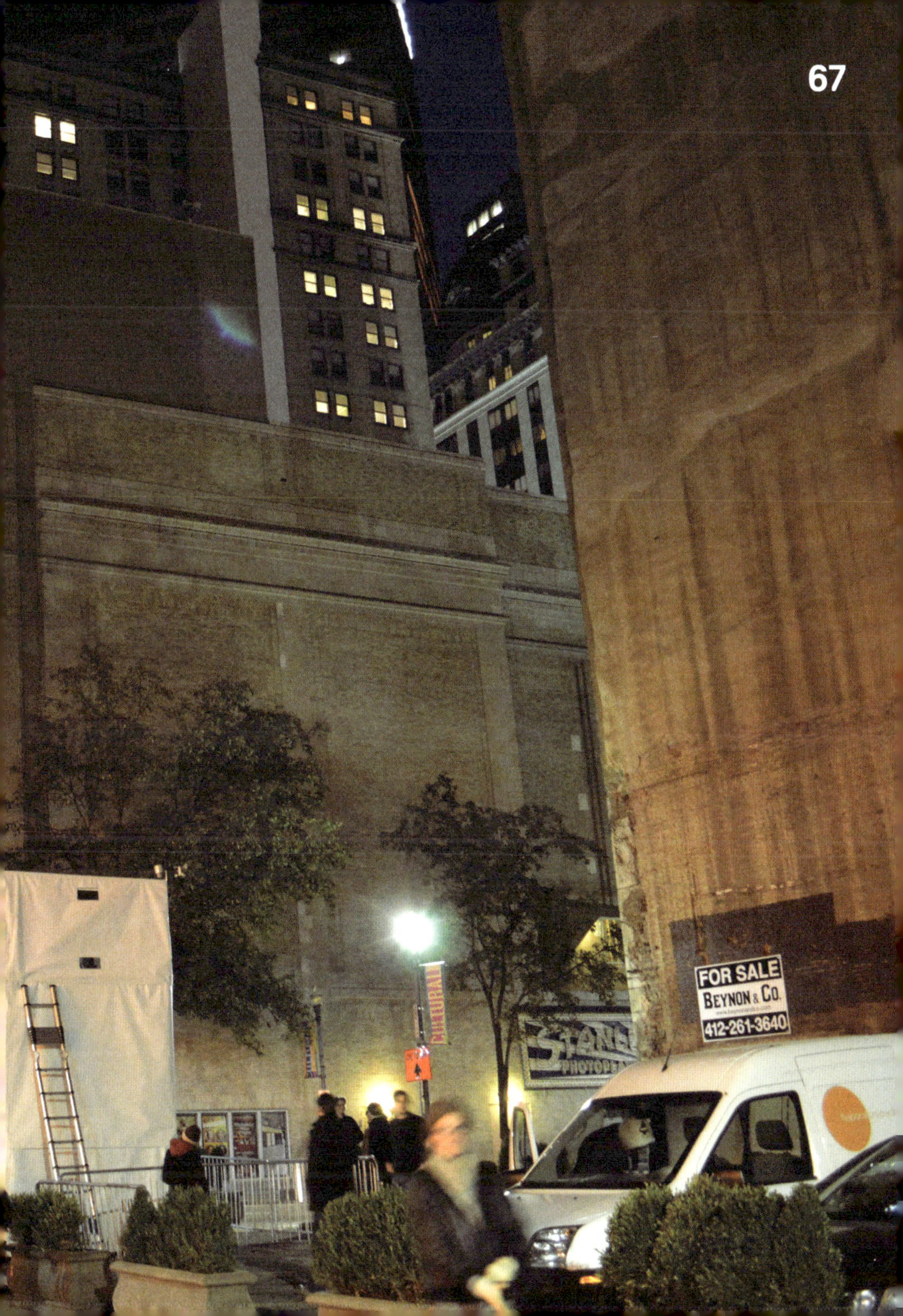
FOR SALE
BEYNON & CO.
www.beynonandco.com
412-261-3640
CENTURIAL

A few years ago, I had the honor of installing my temporary public art project *Particle Falls* in Pittsburgh through The Heinz Endowments's Breathe Project, which had been looking for ways to present particulate pollution to a broader audience. Air quality is often one of the most difficult environmental phenomena to understand, and the ability to see what had been previously invisible can have a profound effect on a public's understanding and experience of their environment. *Particle Falls*, a large-scale light projection work, vividly presents local particulate levels in real time. The project aims to create a link between environment and health—making visible the largely unseen qualities of the air; creating awareness about local data; encouraging communities to monitor environmental conditions with sensors; and providing access to the resources through which to learn more.

Identified in pollution measurements as PM2.5 + PM10 (referring to particulate matter ranging from 2.5 to 10 micron), particulate pollution is a mix of soot, smoke, and other tiny particles in the atmosphere, primarily from sulfur dioxide, nitrogen oxides, and ammonia. Not considered a greenhouse gas, particulate pollution lasts only a few weeks in the atmosphere and can actually have a cooling effect; it scatters and absorbs light, cutting sunlight by up to 10 percent and lowering temperatures. This cooling effect was illustrated dramatically during the three days following September 11, 2001, when planes were grounded across the US. Scientists found that actual temperatures were higher than expected during those three days, and many now attribute this to a lack of contrails—the particulate pollution caused by airplanes.

Particulate pollution is often an indicator of the burning of fossil fuels, and despite a short-term cooling

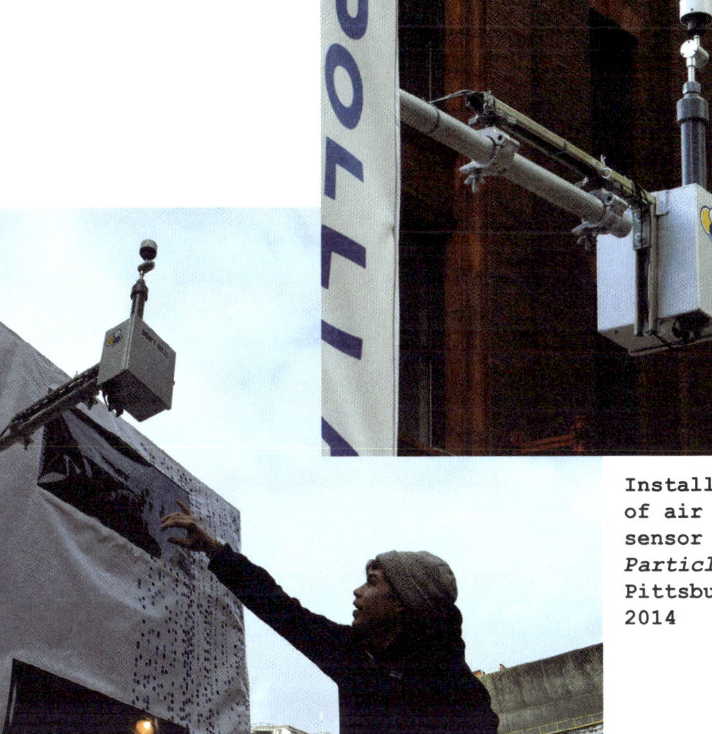

Installation
of air quality
sensor for
*Particle Falls*,
Pittsburgh, PA,
2014



effect, particulates are most likely accompanied by $CO_2$, which contributes to the longer-term effect of global warming. Particulate pollution has also been shown to have a major impact on public health by inducing heart attacks and strokes, causing lung cancer, triggering asthma attacks, and increasing the need for medical care and hospital visits. People with cardiovascular diseases, children, and the elderly are the most vulnerable to the health risks associated with particulate pollution, as are people who suffer from chronic lung disease.

In the 1960s and 1970s, the US saw a significant mobilization of the urban public to address air quality

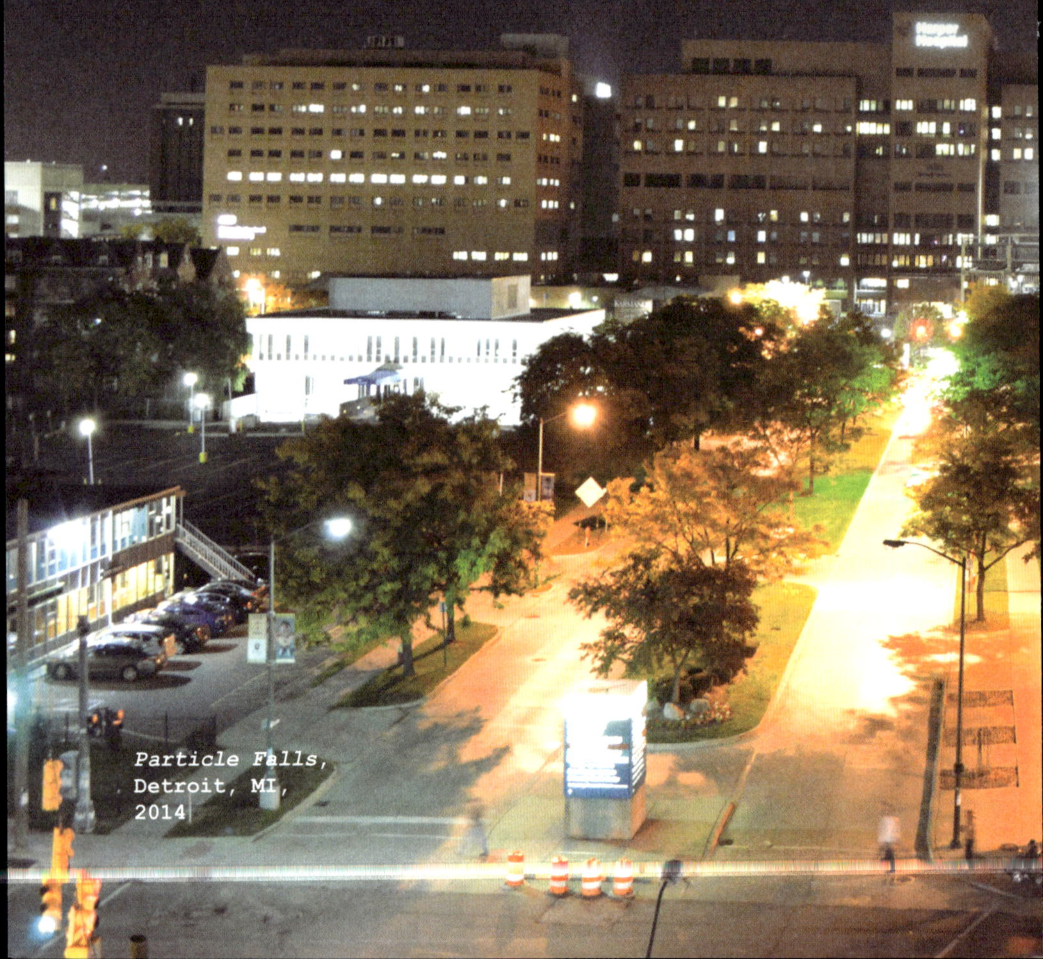
Particle Falls,
Detroit, MI,
2014

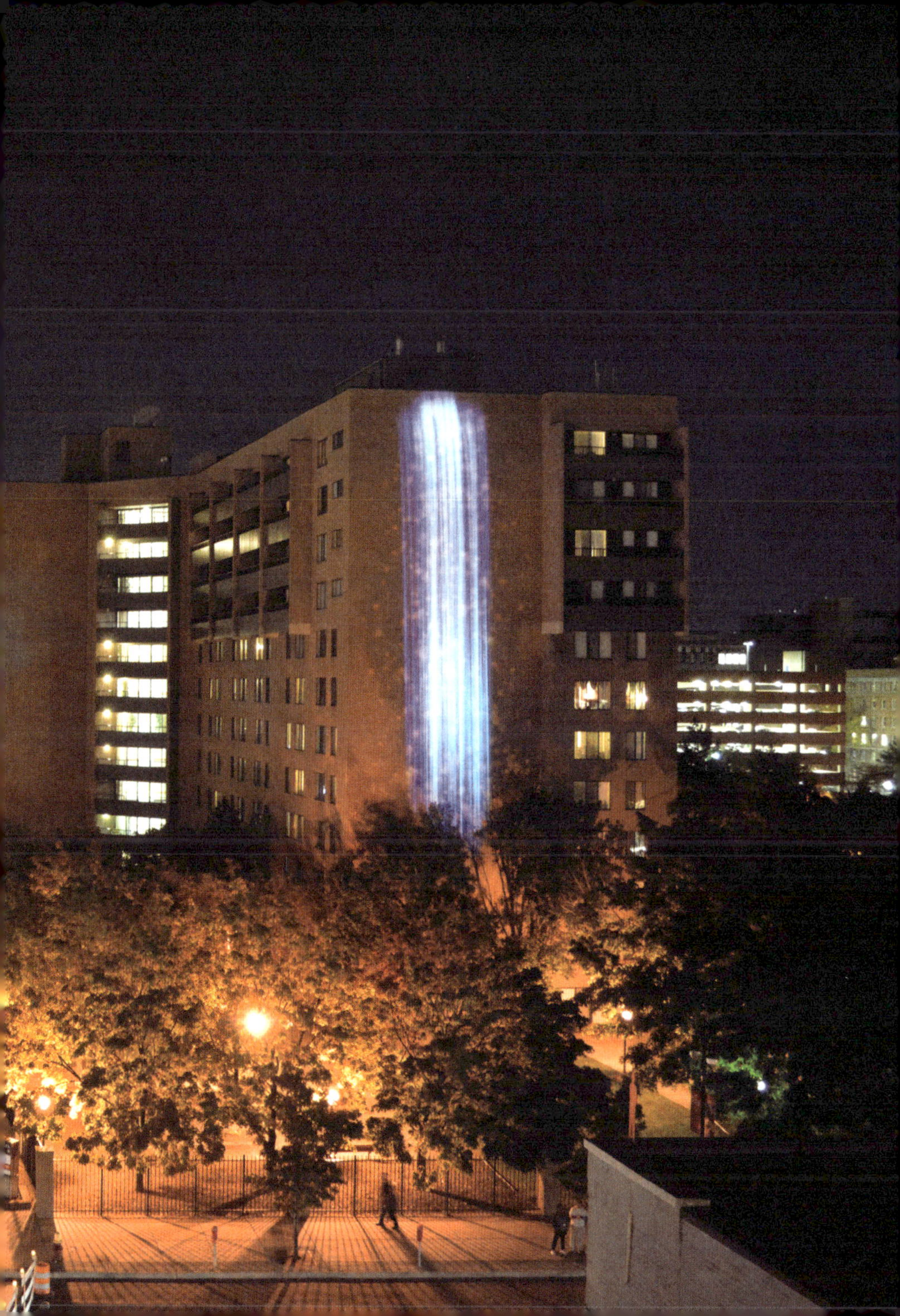

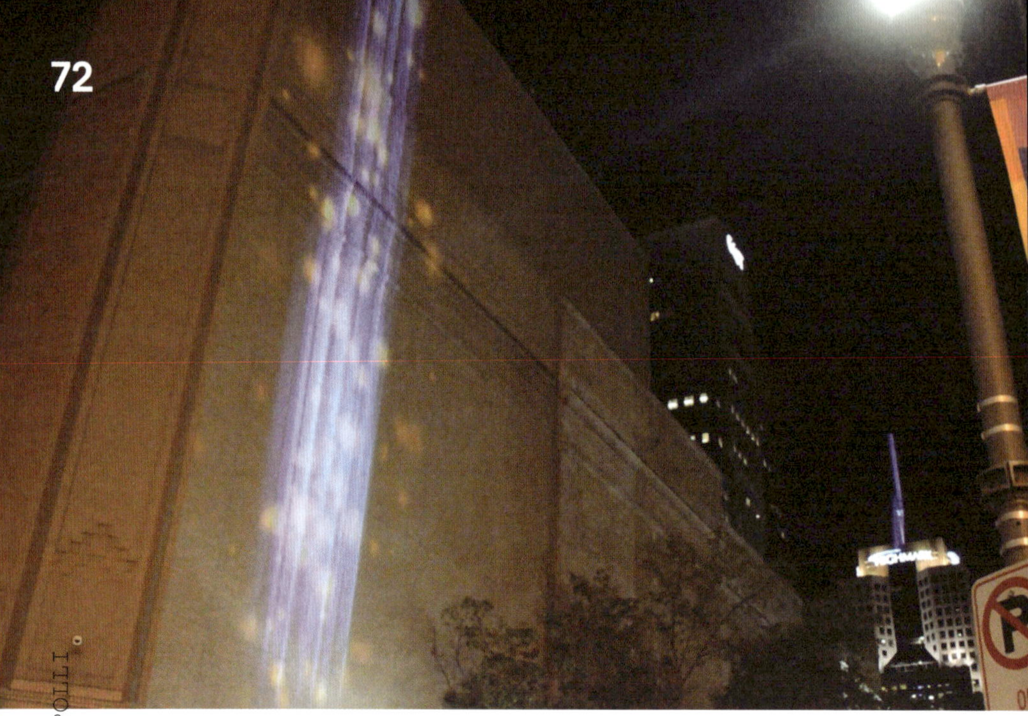



problems. This was due primarily to the widespread use
of coal and the visible manifestations that could be seen.
Smog-covered cities, deadly fogs, and billowing smoke
demanded attention. Regulatory and technological
successes have meant that the more obvious aspects
of poor air quality have largely disappeared, but
many challenges remain. Ozone, particulate matter,
and greenhouse gases contributing to climate change
present significant health and societal problems that
are typically invisible to the public. At the global level,
climate change is all-encompassing. Extreme weather
conditions, water shortages, degraded soils yielding
smaller and less nutritious crops, rapid reduction of
forests and biodiversity, mushrooming public health
emergencies, increased poverty and starvation,
massive migrations, and more—the frequency of these

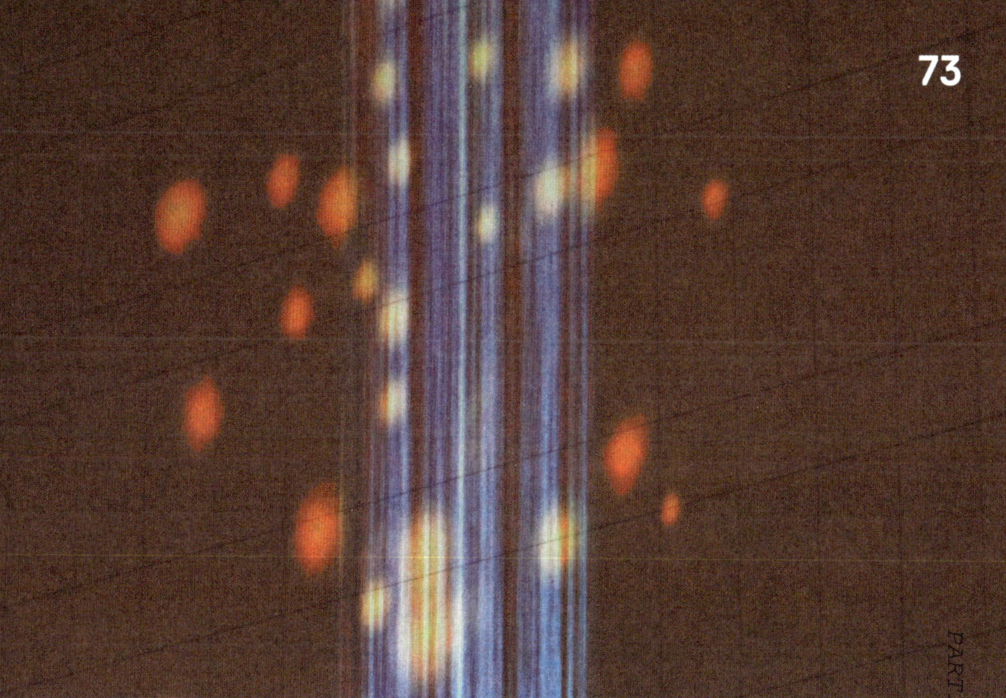



phenomena call for the urgent safeguarding of civil, social, and climate rights and justice. Against this backdrop, it is time to approach climate change from a different perspective by probing below the surface, making the invisible visible.

Despite the unseen nature of air, modern sensors can detect tiny particulate pollution levels in real time. Using large-scale projection technology, *Particle Falls* is a nighttime installation that allows viewers on the street to see current levels of fine particulates cascading down the facade of a public structure. The project relies on an air quality sensing device called a nephelometer, which measures the density of the smallest detectable particle in the air, PM2.5, using a laser scattering technique. The global monitoring of this particle is a relatively recent development in aeronomy, and through a

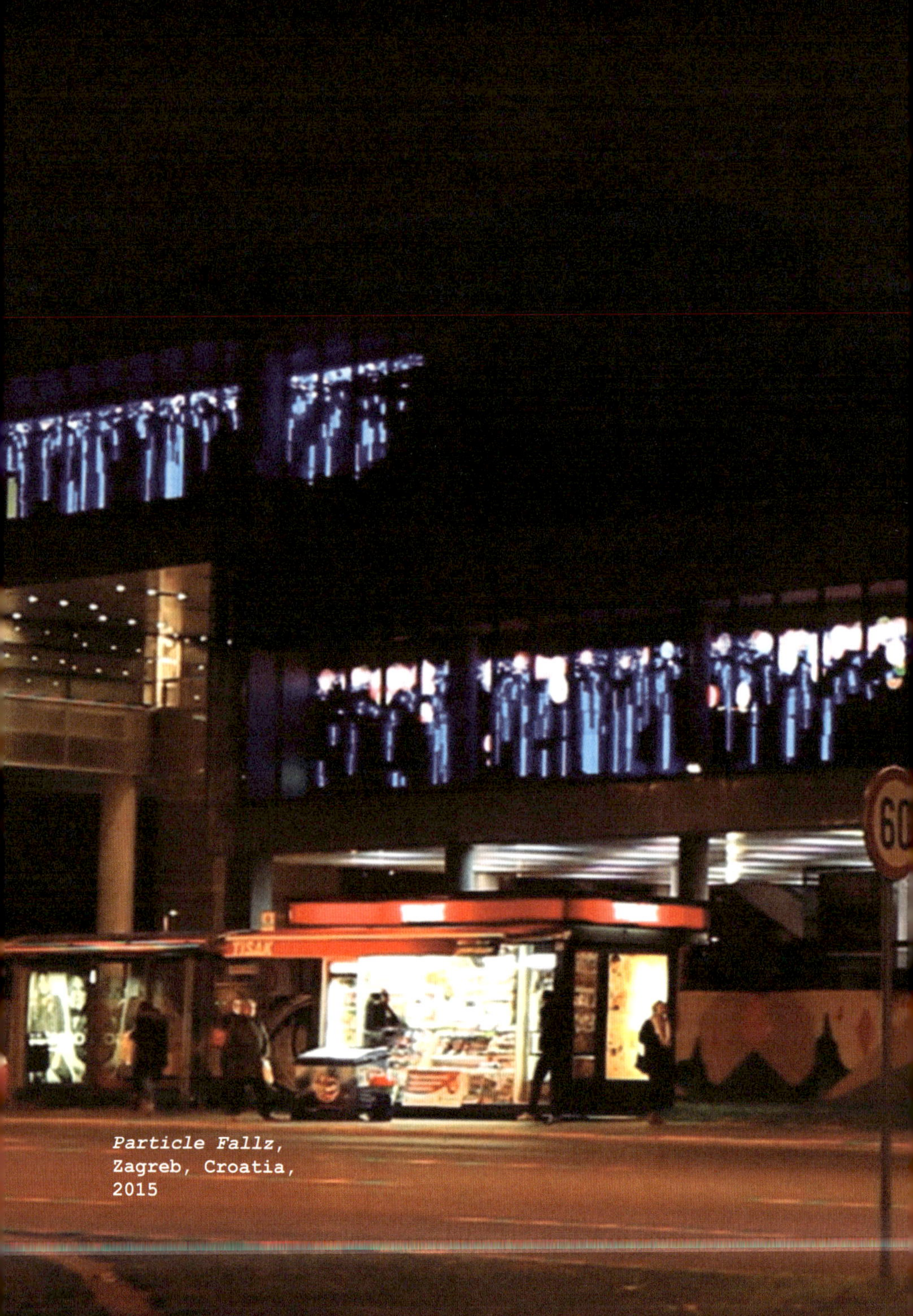

*Particle Fallz,
Zagreb, Croatia,
2015*

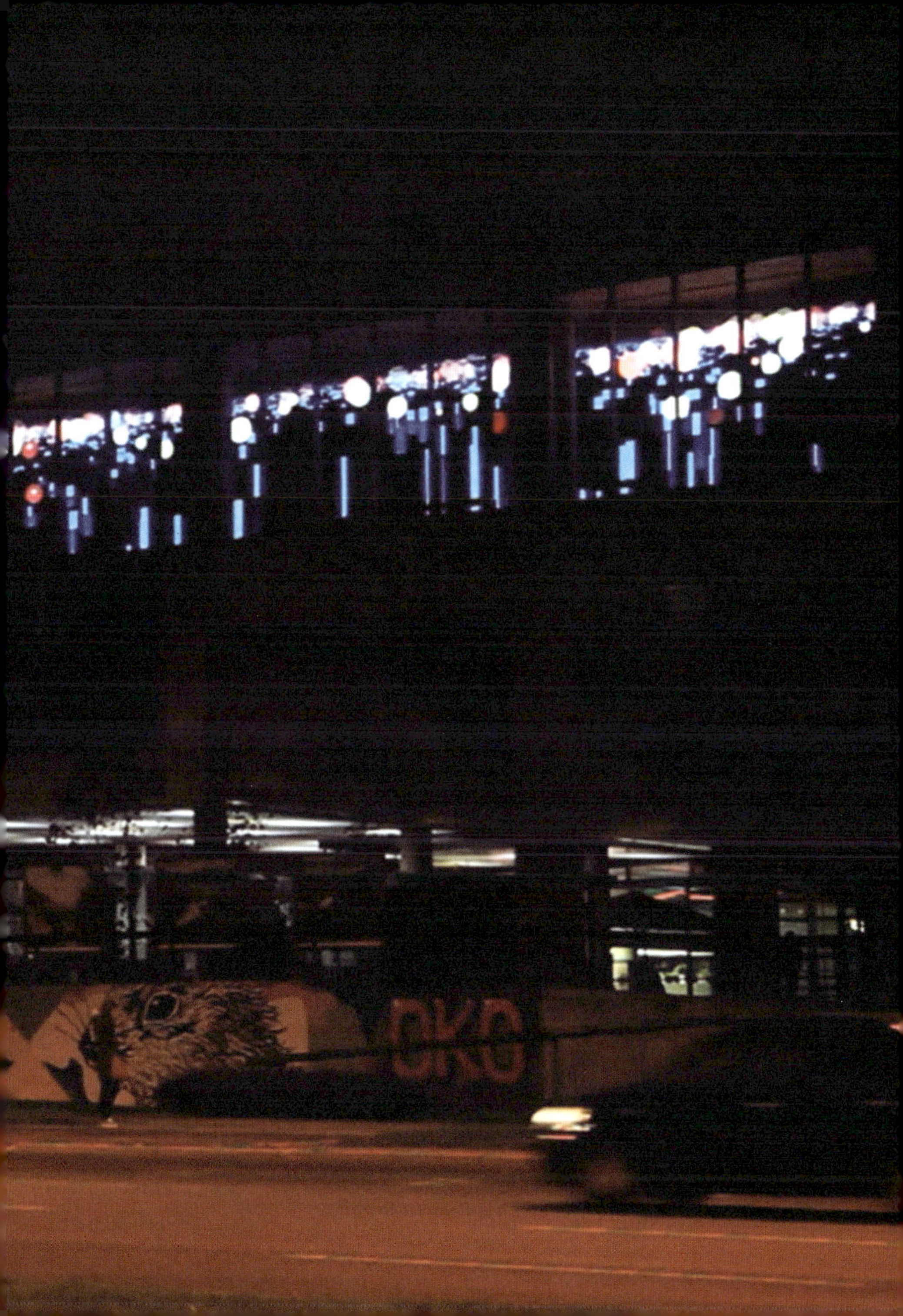

partnership with AirNow, the environmental and air quality monitoring equipment designer MetOne has donated a nephelometer to the *Particle Falls* project.[1]

*Particle Falls* can act as a monitor, an alarm, and a thing of beauty all at the same time by using air pollution as a basis for the dynamic visualization of an otherwise unseen world. The idea of "noise" was also central to the structure of this work. The image of the blue waterfall is computer generated with smooth lines, but when particulate pollution is detected in the air, a pixelated animation appears over the waterfall. This has the effect of a blurring and focusing the image rhythmically as wind sends particles through the air. The impression is that of something quivering or breathing; the image is endowed with a kind of life. Fewer bright particles over the waterfall mean fewer particles in the air, and when more particles are detected, they combine to transform the waterfall into a fireball.

In an address on ephemeral and process-based art, Steven Connor stated: "In much recent art, air has become the marker, not of the difference between art and life, but of the aspiration of art to trespass beyond its assigned precincts, to approach and merge into the condition of 'life.'"[2] Through *Particle Falls*, air-quality data is not merely collected, but it is animated—given life, so to speak—to offer a visual alarm that increases in intensity in concert with the level of pollutants.

Beginning in San Jose, California, in 2009, *Particle Falls* has been presented in many cities including Pittsburgh and Philadelphia; Detroit; Logan, Utah; Charlotte and Raleigh, North Carolina; and Hagen, Germany. I presented a similar project, *Particle Fallz*, on the facade of the Museum of Contemporary Art in Zagreb, Croatia. *Particle Fallz* used three Airbeam sensors created by HabitatMap to detect particulate pollution. Airbeams cost a small fraction of what a professional nephelometer costs, and can even be built and 3D-printed for a lower cost. This is an example of how quickly environmental sensor technology can evolve to become accessible to communities around the world.

In 2015, I presented *Particle Falls* in Paris at the Mona Bismarck American Center in conjunction with the COP21 Paris Climate Conference, where a historic climate agreement was ratified by the UN Framework Convention on Climate Change (UNFCCC)—reaffirming the goal to keep average warming below 2 degrees Celsius. While challenges and obstacles to achieving this goal remain, projects like *Particle Falls* both increase the visibility of local air pollution and confront inequality by arming community members with the ability to see and access the data related to that pollution. Through this, the project also raises public awareness for local advocacy groups, whose voices are too often marginalized within the broader discourse surrounding climate change.

Much of my public work aims to disrupt the ordinary, often drawing attention to invisible changes in a local environment and providing opportunities to discuss related topics such as health and inequality. Many viewers are surprised and want to know more; others are already very aware, but find that the public visualization—such as that of *Particle Falls*—provides a justification for concern and advocacy.

PARTICLE FALLS

Notes

[1] AirNow is an organization that collects data from federal, state, local, and tribal monitoring systems to publish the Air Quality Index (AQI), which presents air quality forecasts and real-time ozone and particle pollution maps for over 400 cities. Data and other information can be found at airnow.gov.

[2] Steven Connor, "Next to Nothing: The Arts of Air," presented at Art Basel, Basel, Switzerland, June 13, 2007.

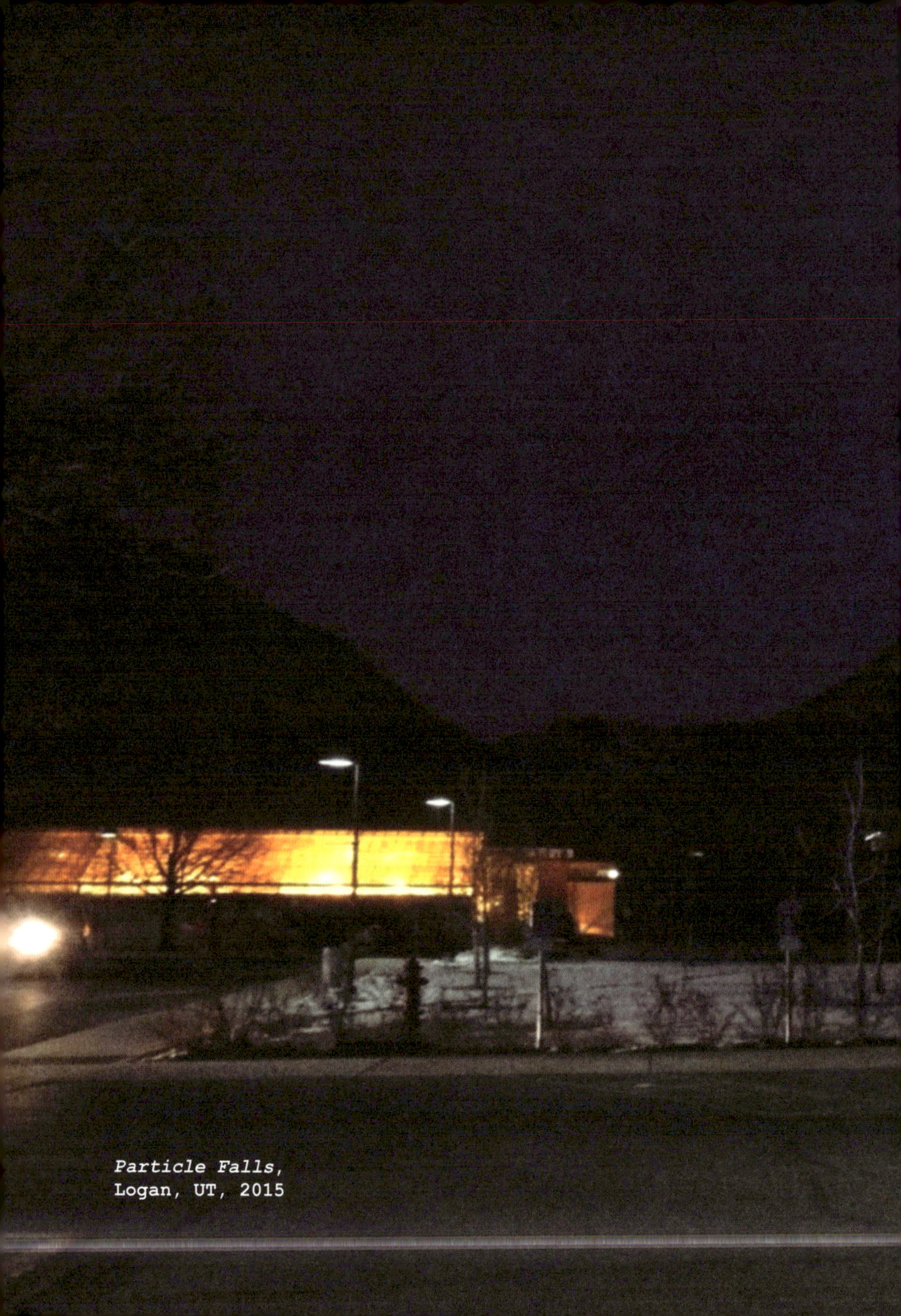

Particle Falls,
Logan, UT, 2015

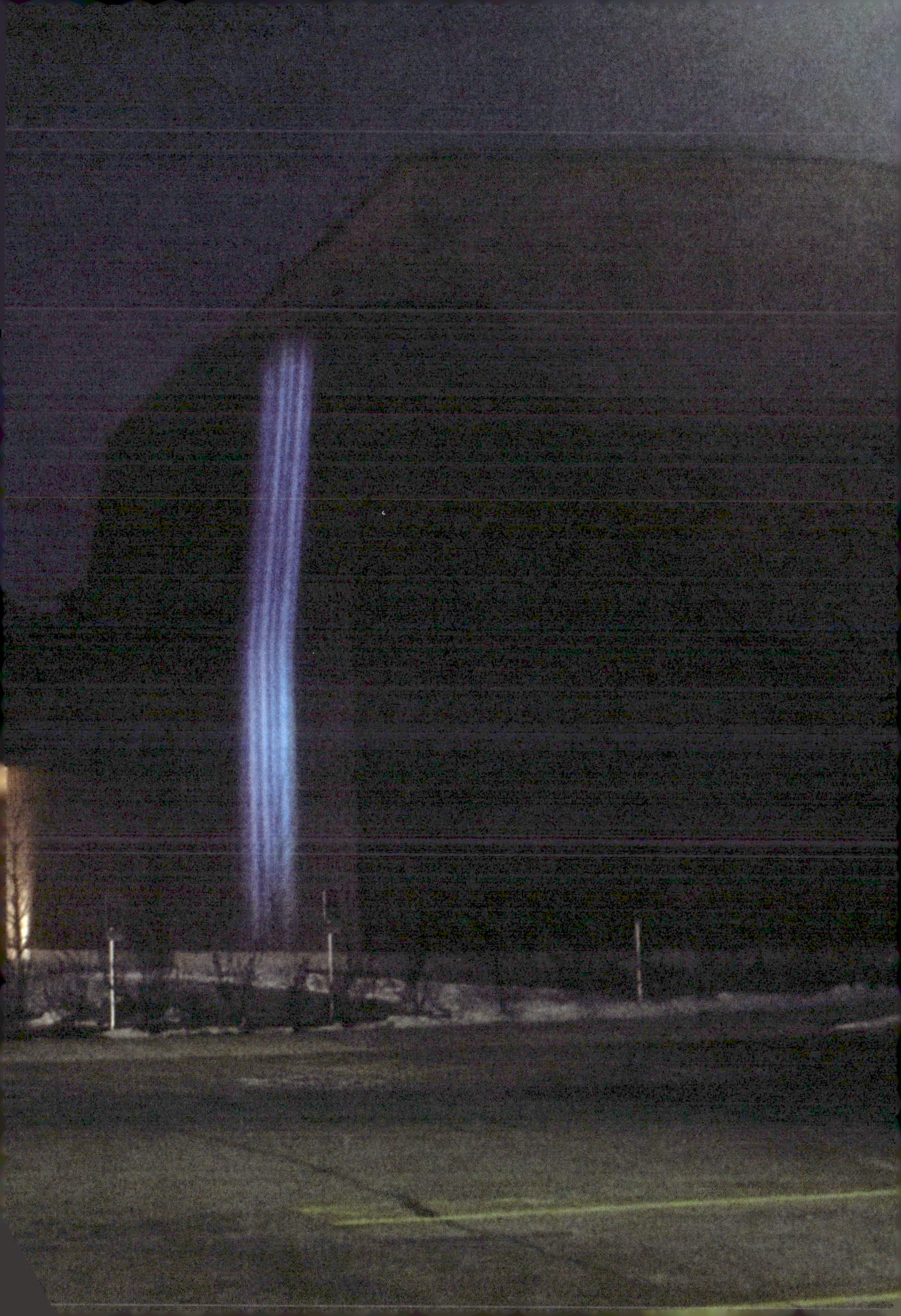

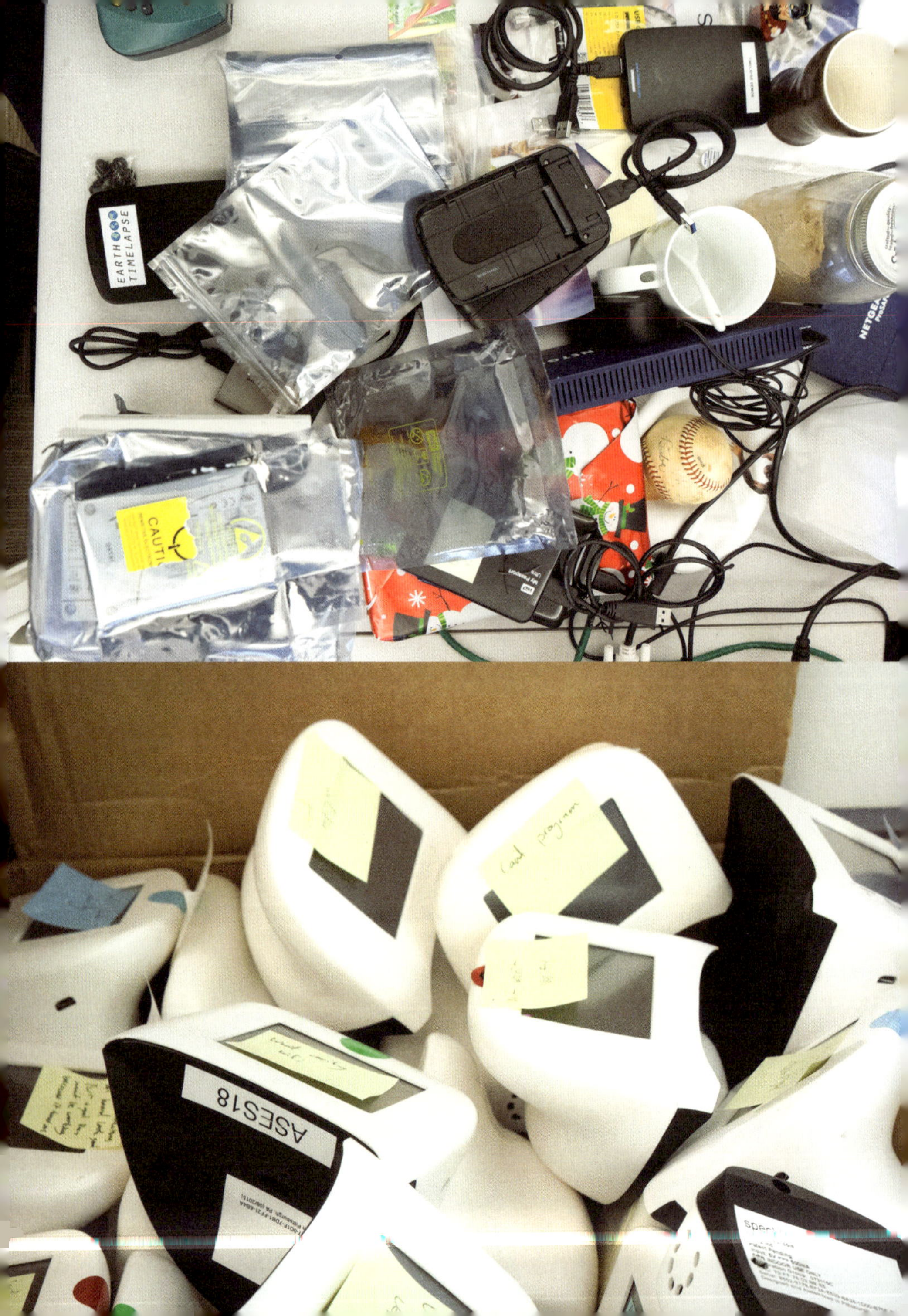

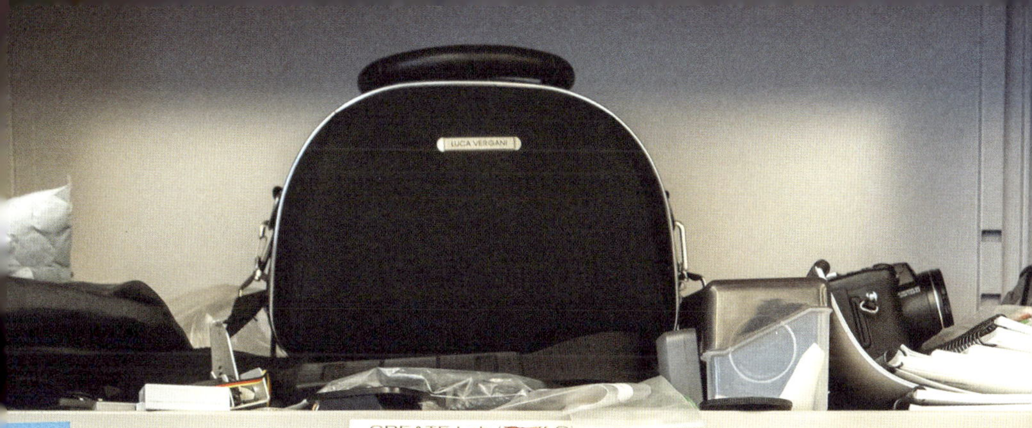

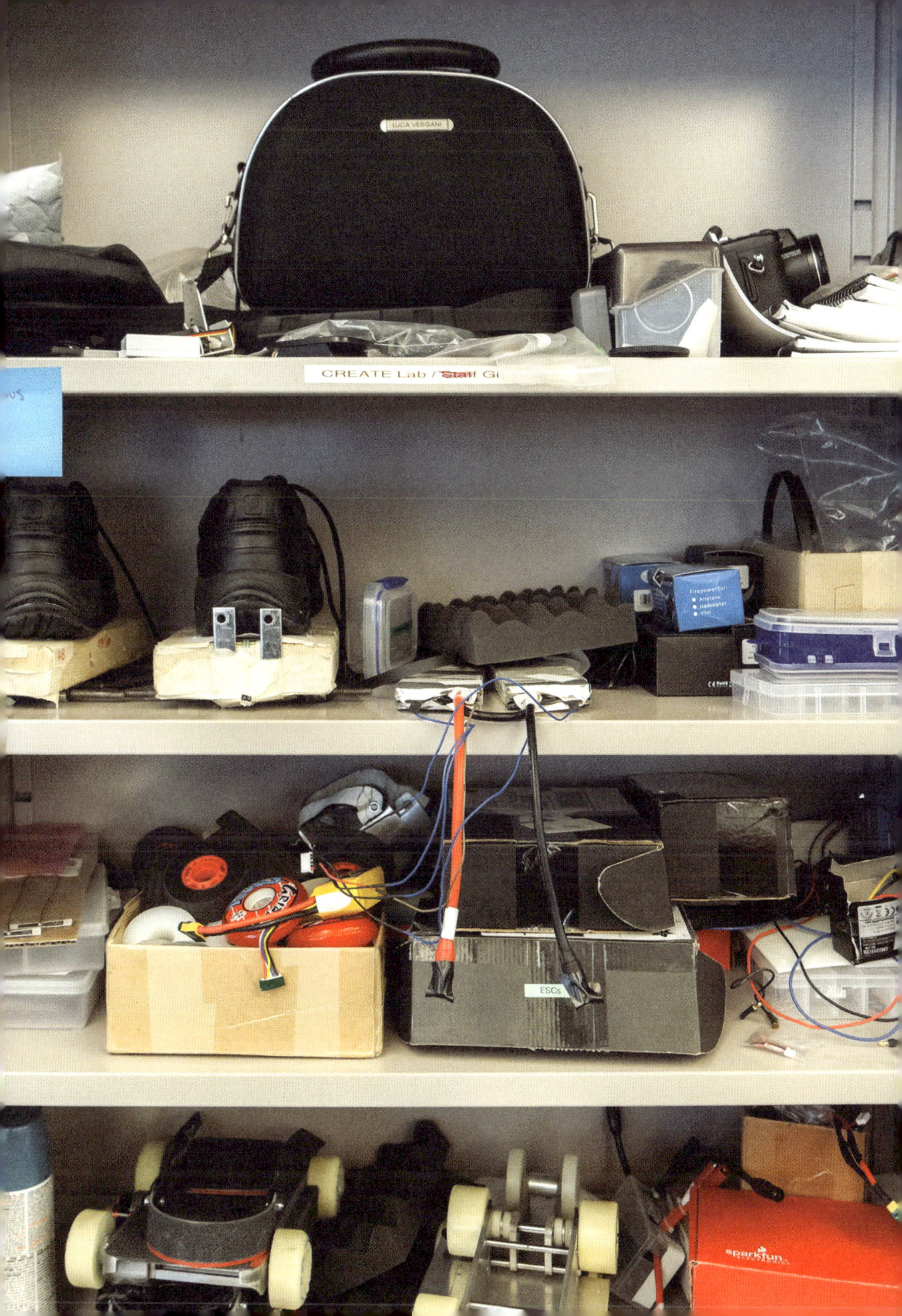

LUCA VERGANI
CREATE Lab / Staff Gi


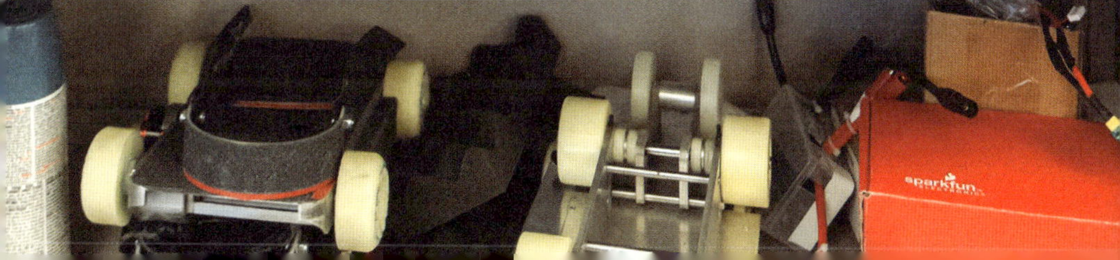

sparkfun

# Andrea Polli in Conversation

with Paul Dille, Yen-Chia Hsu,
& Randy Sargent of the CREATE Lab,
Carnegie Mellon University

with Thaddeus Popovich &
Leah Andrascik of Allegheny
County Clean Air Now

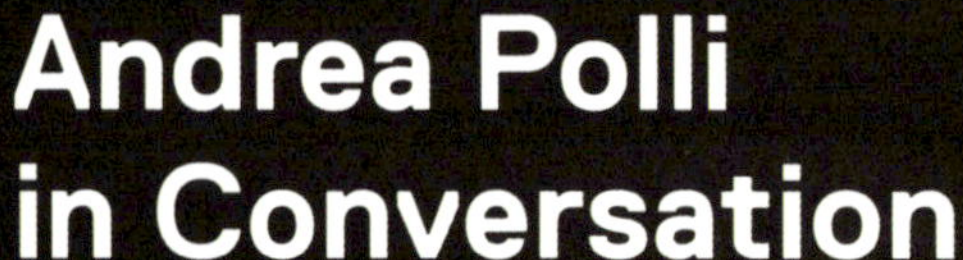

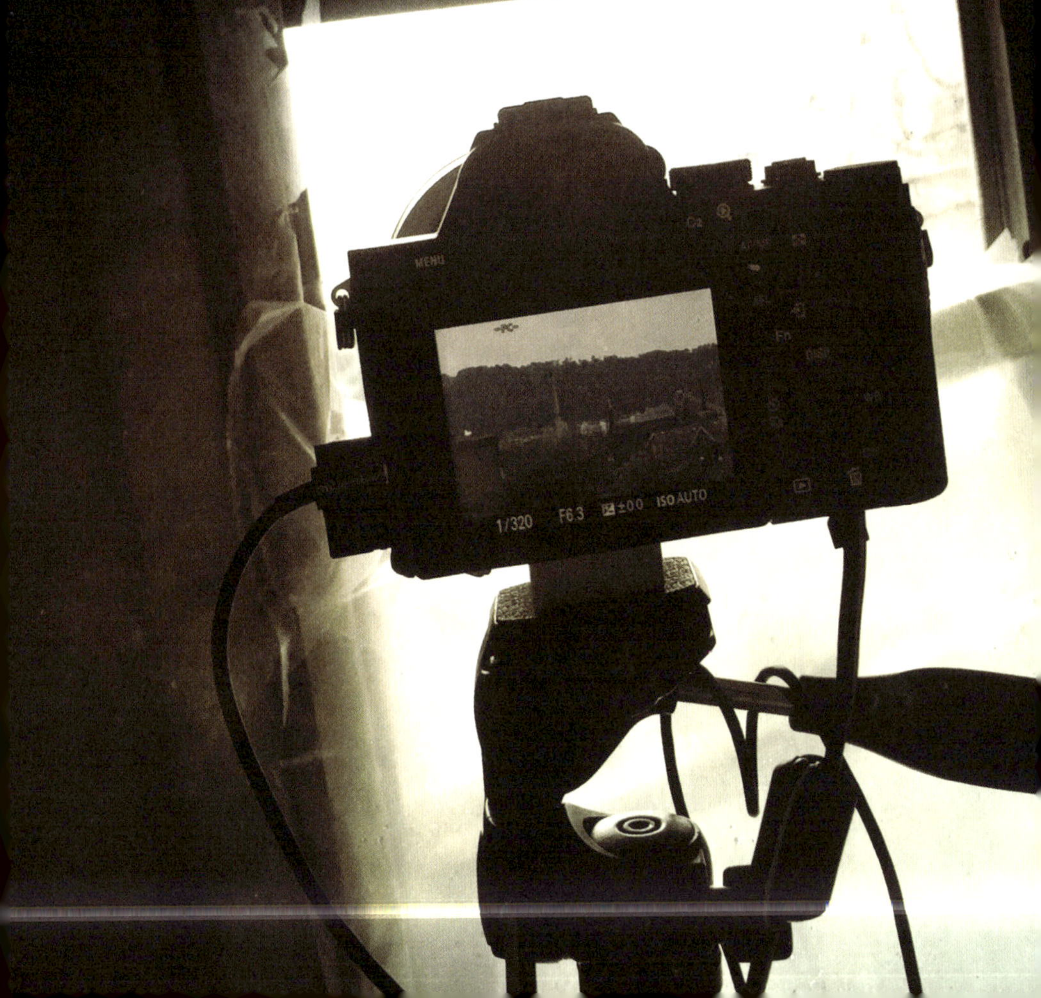

In 2015, members of the Community Robotics, Education, and Technology Empowerment Lab (CREATE Lab) of Carnegie Mellon University collaborated with members of Allegheny County Clean Air Now (ACCAN) to adapt an earlier CREATE Lab project—the Breathe Cam—to monitor air pollution in the community. The result was a web-based air quality monitoring system that allowed community residents to both document and search for sources of smoke emissions.[1]

PAUL DILLE, YEN-CHIA HSU, & RANDY SARGENT
THADDEUS POPOVICH & LEAH ANDRASCIK

For *Hack the Grid*, Andrea Polli spoke with both groups, including three members of the CREATE Lab team who worked on the project—Randy Sargent, Senior Researcher; Paul Dille, Senior Software Programmer; and Yen-Chia Hsu, PhD Candidate in the Robotics Institute at Carnegie Mellon University—and two members of ACCAN, Thaddeus Popovich and Leah Andrascik. The following transcript has been edited for publication.

<u>*Andrea Polli*</u>
*I wonder if we could start by talking about the origins of the Shenango Channel project?*

<u>Randy Sargent</u>
Several years ago, The Heinz Endowments's Breathe Project was interested in the concept of having a haze camera for Pittsburgh that would show how the atmosphere changes over time. This camera would take the same picture of the sky over and over again, so that you can see the differences between a clear day and a day with a lot of particulates in the air.

<u>Paul Dille</u>
We began with just a security camera off the shelf that was designed for years of outdoor usage, but it also had internet connectivity. It would capture the whole horizon once every minute. After additional modifications, it became our first Breathe Cam.

<u>Randy Sargent</u>
Paul was able to set up the time lapse to take hundreds of megapixels per frame; we developed a way to let you zoom in and stream to the computer. It's the equivalent

of Google Maps. If you look at the satellite view of Google Maps, you see a picture of the earth that you can't possibly download. It would take months. When you zoom in, though, it sends you the pieces of the picture at the resolution you need. We had developed a technology in the Lab for doing that with zoomable video.

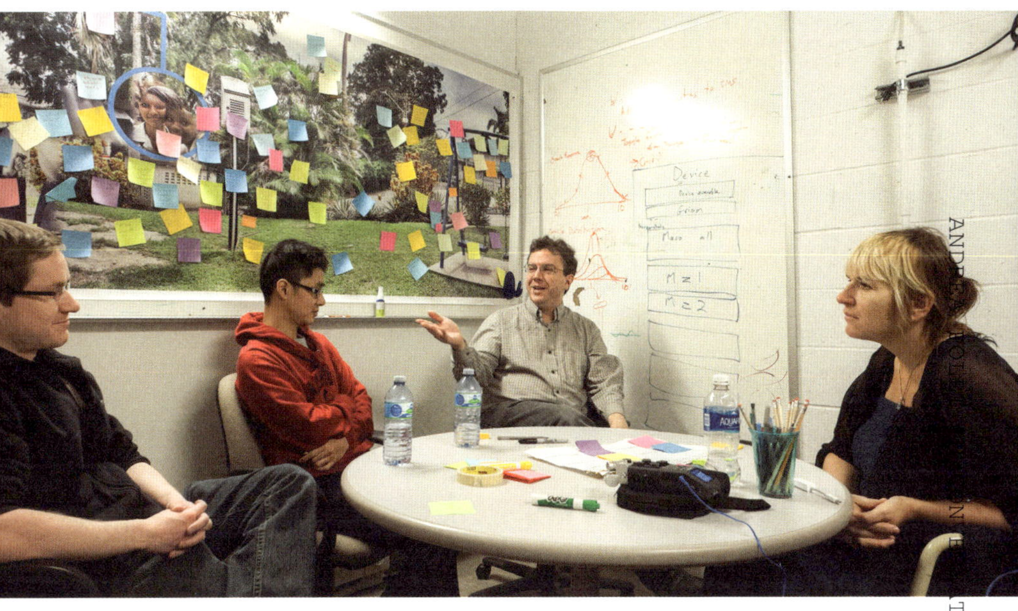

From left to right:
Paul Dille, Yen-Chia Hsu, Randy Sargent, Andrea Polli

*Andrea Polli*
*Then you adapted this camera for what would become the Shenango Channel?*

Randy Sargent
Yes, Paul took this technology and extended it to capture images every few seconds, and Josh Schapiro from the Lab built a new camera that was better suited to capturing industrial sources.

PAUL DILLE, YEN–CHIA HSU, & RANDY SARGENT
THADDEUS POPOVICH & LEAH ANDRASCIK

*Andrea Polli*
*Let me back up. Why did you want to do that?*

Randy Sargent
With the CREATE Lab, we try to be in service of the community. One of the things that was interesting to us when we published the Breathe Cam online is that when you start zooming into different places around Pittsburgh, you would see not only the overall haze, but also individual industrial sources. That's when we got connected to a group from one of the communities impacted by industrial sources, the Allegheny County Clean Air Now (ACCAN).

The Shenango Coke Works on Neville Island in Allegheny County took coal and turned it into coke, which is the primary fuel in the production of steel. The process liberates lots of volatile organic compounds, some of which are burned on site for heat as part of the oven. Some are flared—burned intentionally so that the raw gases cannot escape into the environment. Sometimes it's a clean flare, and sometimes it's very smoky. Many times we observed "fugitive" emissions— unplanned pollution events from the plant, with causes including leaking doors or inoperative venting. It's complicated because you would get emissions and

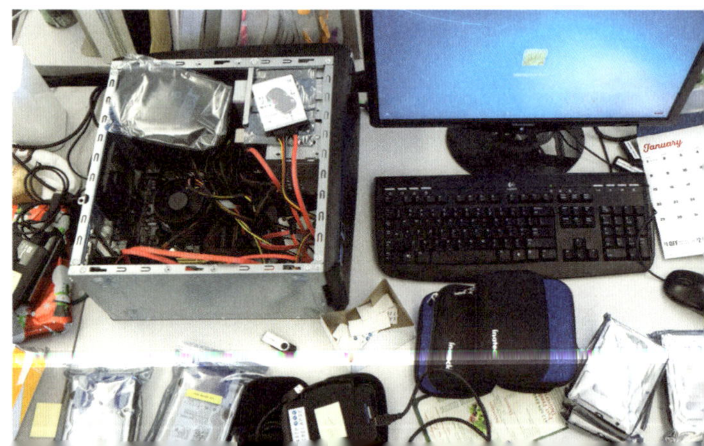

different smells at different times. The first camera was pointed at the plant from the attic of one of the ACCAN members, Leah Andrascik.

Now, suddenly, the whole world can see pictures. Once the camera was deployed, we were surprised by the stories that we saw in the imagery, and how it visualized the experiences and anecdotes of people in the area. We really see the Shenango Channel as a partnership with ACCAN. They helped design it.

Thaddeus Popovich

I think our initial connection with the CREATE Lab was with the smoke reading, or emissions evaluation, that we did overlooking the Ohio River across from the Shenango facility. I was an emissions evaluator along with some others.

*Andrea Polli*
*Why did you decide to become a smoke reader?*

Thaddeus Popovich

We're legal weapons, you might say. We can report our findings to the health department, and it's logged as legal data. I was a board member of GASP (Group Against Smog and Pollution), which supports the smoke reading project. Basically, smoke reading is connecting your eyes and your brain to what you're witnessing. You're able to discern the opacity of smoke, whether it is black or white.

Leah Andrascik

I got involved with the group after my son was born five weeks premature. Shortly after his birth, I read in the newspaper that there was a connection between air pollution and poor birth outcomes. It was kind of a light bulb moment for me.

Thaddeus Popovich

I moved back to the area eight years ago. I chose to live, unwittingly, a half a mile across the river from the second largest pollution source in the area, as it turned out. Allegheny County, southwest Pennsylvania, has the dirtiest air east of California according to the American Lung Association. We get a report card every year: F's all the way across the board. With ACCAN, I'd say we've become more of an activist group than not. We get into street theater. We're willing to push people's buttons. We've never been arrested, though.

*Andrea Polli*
*How did you connect with ACCAN?*

Randy Sargent
Two people in the Lab, myself and Beatrice Dias, took GASP classes on how to look at smoke and assess it as a violation, and it turned out that several ACCAN members had been doing this for years. We went to one of their smoke-reading events, and we brought along a camera, which we set up for two hours.

Paul Dille
The first time we ran it through our software, it was clear you could tell the difference between steam and actual smoke emissions. We had a picture every five seconds at that point. It excited everyone, because we realized that we could correlate what the residents were experiencing. They would report a smell, but whenever an inspector would come out, they would sometimes say, "Oh, I don't know. They were paving the street here." With the Shenango Channel, you could tie all those data points together: the physical person smelling it, the particulate sensor we also deployed, and then

the camera. This was an unprecedented correlation of information for them.

*Andrea Polli*
*Prior to that, air quality analysts would get trained to write in a book, "This is the color I see, this is what I smell, this is the time," and so on?*

Randy Sargent
What's interesting is that everyone was trained to look at the main stack, which was also being monitored continuously. You could then use the Freedom of Information Act and find the actual data because it was submitted to the health department.

But we found on the camera is that the most interesting stuff wasn't coming out of that stack. Fugitive emissions would come at random from different places. Different ovens would be at different phases. Sometimes it would come when they were loading the coal in. Sometimes it would come when they were taking coke out. Sometimes it would come in between, and you'd have these different emissions indicating that either something was going wrong or someone was getting sloppy.

You can find an event, play through it fast, and see the big cloud of smoke. Then you can go back and find the exact frame where it started coming out. That was an important part of the story. For people in the community, when you can actually point to the image of something happening, it is much harder to argue against.

Through looking at related air samples, we were able to show that when the smell was the worst, the concentrations of the bad stuff in the air were five to ten times higher than they normally were. Things like benzene were getting to be significant. People from the

PAUL DILLE, YEN-CHIA HSU, & RANDY SARGENT
THADDEUS POPOVICH & LEAH ANDRASCIK

plant would say, "Oh, it's just hydrogen sulfide. It smells bad, but it's not bad for you." We now had data which indicated that's not the case.

Leah Andrascik
Up to this point, I had sent complaints to the health department for about two years, and we had gone to the in-person meetings. I had become so frustrated with the lack of results that I was excited that somebody who had some clout behind their name was listening to us and genuinely wanted to help. When we were first looking for a location for the Breathe Cam, I took a cellphone picture of a really hazy day and I sent it to Randy. He wrote back and asked for a picture with more of the horizon, and from a higher vantage point. When I was attempting to do that, I went up into our attic and realized that you could see the battery of the coke plant from there. That was what sparked the idea to put the camera in our attic.

*Andrea Polli*
*Cool. Is it still up there now?*

Leah Andrascik
Yep. We dubbed that the "citizen's camera."

*Andrea Polli*
*The community was able to make quite an impact with all of this. How did that play out?*

Paul Dille
Several community members became much more comfortable with speaking out about Shenango. Some wanted to be anonymous initially, but as time went on they were willing to be interviewed. Just seeing that

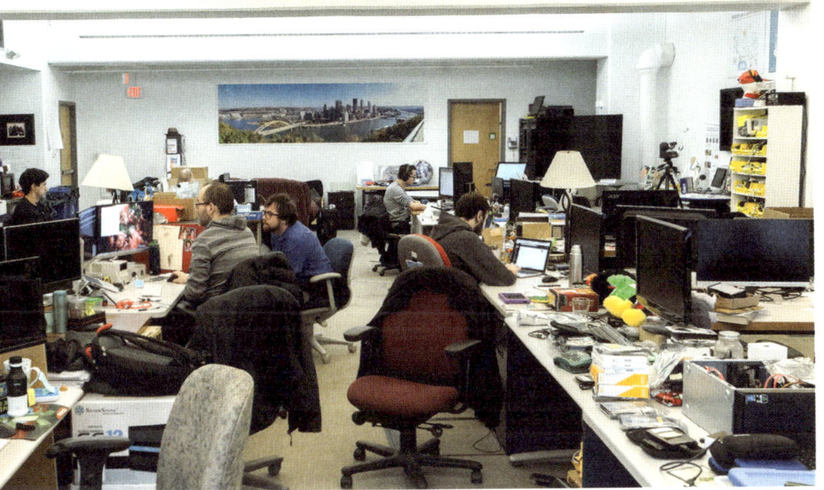



growth in different community members was great. It was a process of becoming empowered, which to me was very heartwarming.

Randy Sargent
And beyond the Shenango Channel, the community was creative in expressing their growing frustration. They did an interesting event where they invited the press to Shenango, and then gave the plant the "Closed Window Award." This was meant to say, "It's spring now. It's warm. We should be opening our windows and we can't!" In response, someone from the plant wrote a letter to the editor that was published, claiming that smells are subjective and that there were many other industrial things going on—as well as other things that can smell, like repairing a roof. They implied that the people who were complaining didn't really know what they're talking about.

*Andrea Polli*
*That's why the people need the scientific process.*

PAUL DILLE, YEN-CHIA HSU, & RANDY SARGENT
THADDEUS POPOVICH & LEAH ANDRASCIK

Randy Sargent

In November 2015, ACCAN hosted a large community meeting with more than a hundred people. They had invited Dave Arnold, the acting head of air protection for EPA Region III Air Protection Division in Philadelphia. People from the community talked about their personal experiences, and we showed videos from the Shenango Channel. Paul Dille had done important work to first let people find an individual instance of smoke, draw a box around it, and make an animated GIF. That was really popular. These were being mailed to the EPA and emailed to each other to put on Facebook. And then Yen-Chia Hsu made a way of doing this automatically.

Yen-Chia Hsu

We ran small workshops with people in ACCAN to document the smoke in the images. We had a tool in our system that allowed users to go into a video, find the moment when the smoke appeared, and manually mark a window. The tool can then generate an animated image, which is really powerful because people can see how bad the emission is. But there was a problem: we had a lot of videos to search.

Randy Sargent

A year's worth.

*Andrea Polli*

*Every five seconds of a year.*

Yen-Chia Hsu

Searching all of these was basically impossible, so I wrote software for the computer to search for smoke emissions in videos. This algorithm can output a lot of animated images for the community to then look at and select from. We were able to present images of the worst fugitive emissions to the EPA and the local health department. Before this, the community could share their personal experiences, but they couldn't provide scientific evidence.

Now they have the images, which we can combine with other information. For instance, we can say, "Okay, now wind blows this way. It's definite that smoke emission comes here." The community can tell this story to the EPA and actually change the attitude of the government.

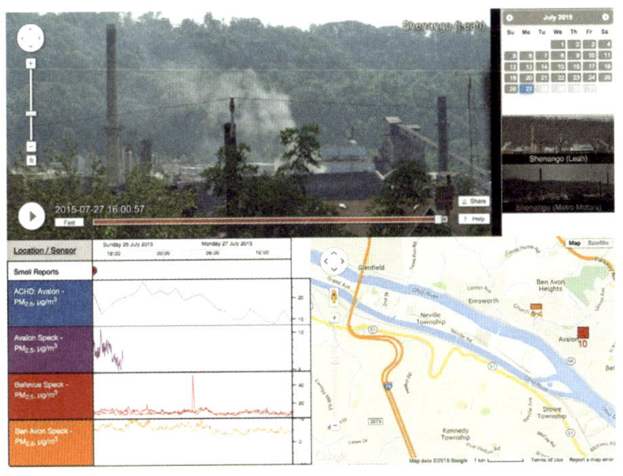

Shenango Channel website, showing a fugitive emission from July 27, 2015



_Andrea Polli_
_Really? What happened when they saw it?_

Yen-Chia Hsu
Dave Arnold from the EPA pointed at the screen at the meeting and said, "This is totally unacceptable."

Randy Sargent
It was written up in the _Pittsburgh Post-Gazette_ the next day. They quoted him: "totally unacceptable."

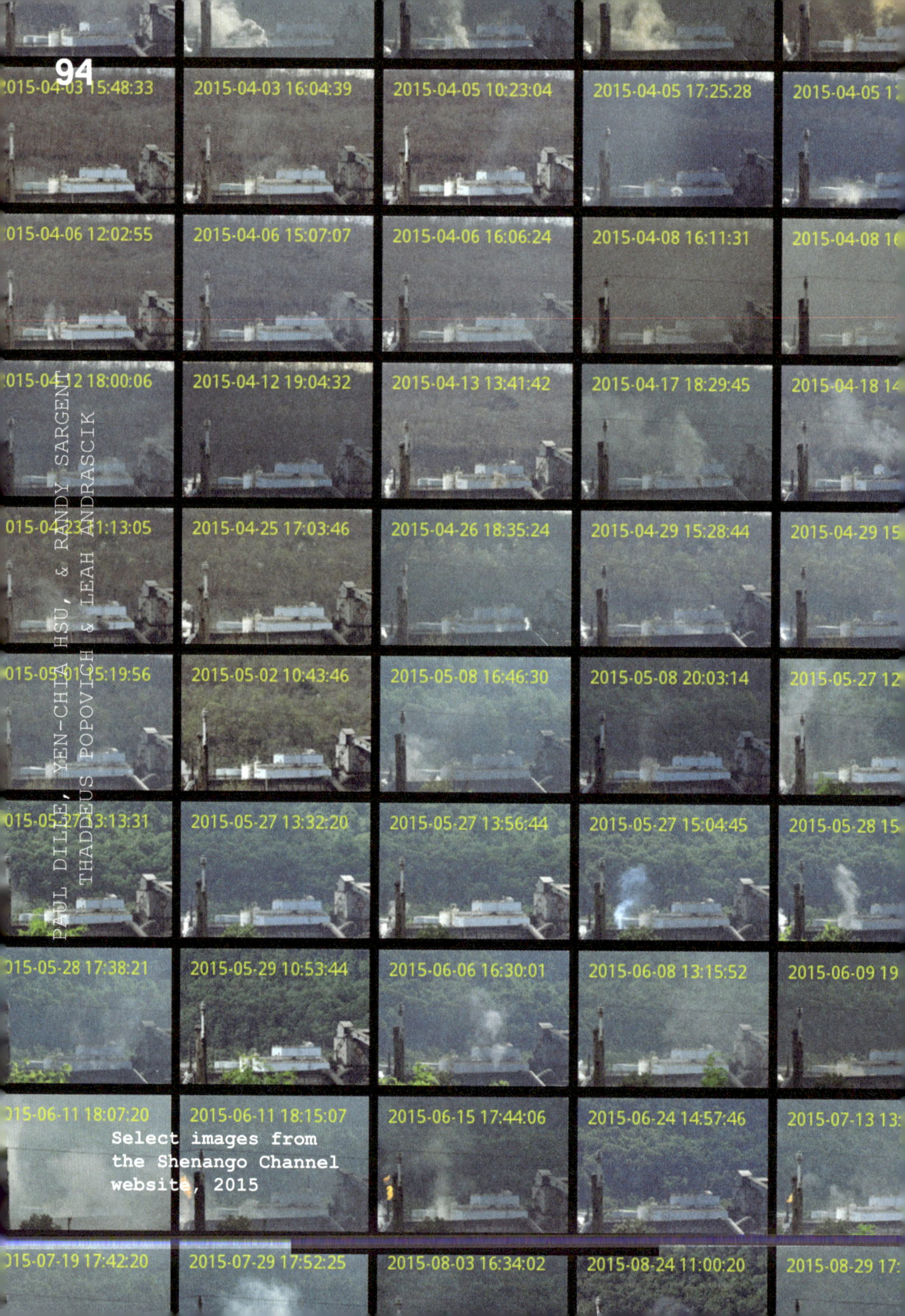
94
PAUL DILLE, YEN-CHIA HSU, & RANDY SARGENT
THADDEUS POPOVICH & LEAH ANDRASCIK
Select images from
the Shenango Channel
website, 2015
2015-04-03 15:48:33
2015-04-03 16:04:39
2015-04-05 10:23:04
2015-04-05 17:25:28
2015-04-05 1
2015-04-06 12:02:55
2015-04-06 15:07:07
2015-04-06 16:06:24
2015-04-08 16:11:31
2015-04-08 16
2015-04-12 18:00:06
2015-04-12 19:04:32
2015-04-13 13:41:42
2015-04-17 18:29:45
2015-04-18 14
2015-04-23 11:13:05
2015-04-25 17:03:46
2015-04-26 18:35:24
2015-04-29 15:28:44
2015-04-29 15
2015-05-01 15:19:56
2015-05-02 10:43:46
2015-05-08 16:46:30
2015-05-08 20:03:14
2015-05-27 12
2015-05-27 13:13:31
2015-05-27 13:32:20
2015-05-27 13:56:44
2015-05-27 15:04:45
2015-05-28 15
2015-05-28 17:38:21
2015-05-29 10:53:44
2015-06-06 16:30:01
2015-06-08 13:15:52
2015-06-09 19
2015-06-11 18:07:20
2015-06-11 18:15:07
2015-06-15 17:44:06
2015-06-24 14:57:46
2015-07-13 13
2015-07-19 17:42:20
2015-07-29 17:52:25
2015-08-03 16:34:02
2015-08-24 11:00:20
2015-08-29 17

Leah Andrascik

Yen-Chia had compiled the camera images for any time there was black smoke coming out, and he had it on a big screen in front of the audience and there would be one image, then two, then four, and so on. It kept expanding! Incidentally, the screen was set up directly in front of where David Arnold was seated.

Thaddeus Popovich

He stood up at one point after he saw this mosaic of egregious events. He said, "This is totally unacceptable." It was like the shock heard around the world—at least our world anyway. DTE Energy, who owns Shenango, certainly did not like this kind of exposure.

*Andrea Polli*
*What happened next?*

Randy Sargent
After that community meeting with Dave Arnold, there was another op-ed from Shenango that effectively said, "Just because it looks bad doesn't mean it's actually bad for you." But it was a hard sell to point at an ugly brown or yellow or black cloud and convince people that it wasn't unhealthy, that it was perfectly fine. We saw a very different message just in the space of less than a year.

*Andrea Polli*
*Now the plant is shut down. Is there a direct correlation with what happened with the Shenango Channel?*

Randy Sargent
The project we undertook with ACCAN to create the Shenango Channel hoped to help them find a voice that

PAUL DILLE, YEN-CHIA HSU, & RANDY SARGENT
THADDEUS POPOVICH & LEAH ANDRASCIK

could no longer be ignored. And I think together we successfully reached that goal.

What I saw in the imagery and data is that there were times when Shenango appeared to run cleanly, and times when it was very dirty. Furthermore—and this was consistent with earlier observations from the community—it was more often dirty on the weekends, which led us to the question: why couldn't Shenango be operated more cleanly all the time?

DTE Energy announced about a month after the community meeting that the plant was shutting down for economic reasons. They didn't mention the Shenango Channel or ACCAN in their press release, but I've been in touch with an industrial expert who wonders if DTE might be reluctant to publicly admit to concerns about health impacts from Shenango—which is easy to understand when you count up the excess deaths and asthma in the area.[2]

But at a place and time with a dwindling supply of industrial and manufacturing jobs, Shenango's closing is truly unfortunate for the people who worked there. This situation also feeds the false dichotomy of jobs or environment. I want a world where we have both. We saw evidence that the plant could be operated cleanly. Perhaps that takes more effort.

*Andrea Polli*
*With this focus social impacts, I think that the CREATE Lab is transforming what's happening in computer science and engineering. From your perspective, what are some of the things that you need to do differently, and how does that transform practice in the field? What are the skills that community groups should be building and thinking about to most effectively collaborate?*

Yen-Chia Hsu

I think one really important concept is scientists as citizens. Historically, when we haven't had the technology to advocate for environmental improvements, we have relied on representatives that can present the people's ideas. Citizens cannot usually work directly with that person, though. I think it's important for citizens to have their own data in their hands, because when they have data, they have the power to say something. They can directly influence their representative government.

All communities have their own characteristics, and to work with them, we learn to adapt to how they work. I consider my role as a supporter—almost like IT support. The community is the expert.

Paul Dille

To add to that, as a computer scientist you can't directly solve specific social problems; they may be too unique to that community. But you can build a repertoire of guidelines or recipes that can be applied to that situation. For the Shenango Channel, we have now a process in place: the data you can collect, how you can organize it, visualize it, and send it out. If you're a scientist, you can build generalized systems. Communities should be able to take aspects of those tools and apply them to their specific needs.

Yen-Chia Hsu

This is a case where community experts and computer engineers built a tool that armed its citizens with the power to tell the truth. This is something that is critical for computer engineers to consider. Typically, they might focus a lot on the implementation of the product and little on its social impacts. With this project, we

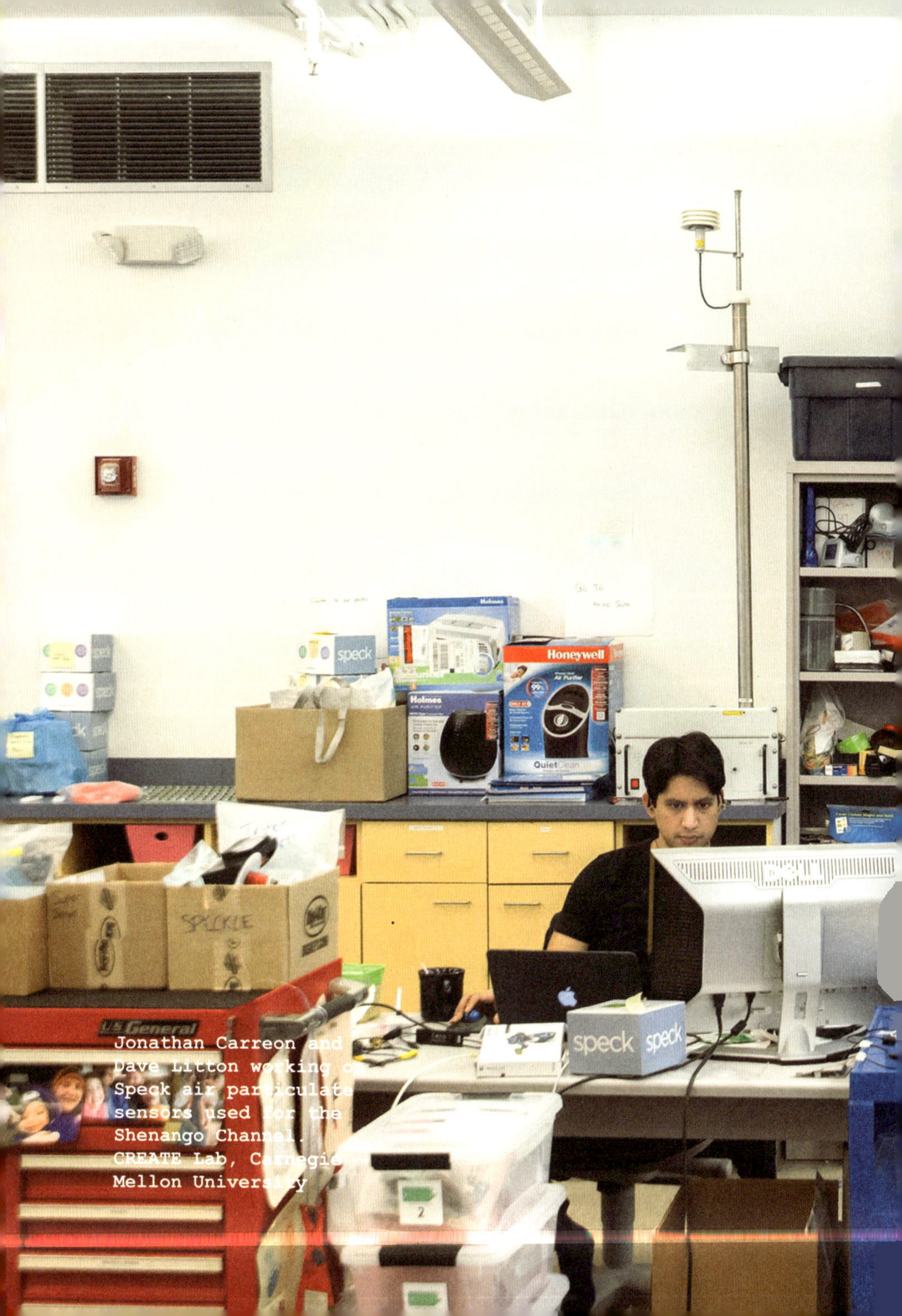

Jonathan Carreon and
Dave Litton working on
Speck air particulate
sensors used for the
Shenango Channel.
CREATE Lab, Carnegie
Mellon University

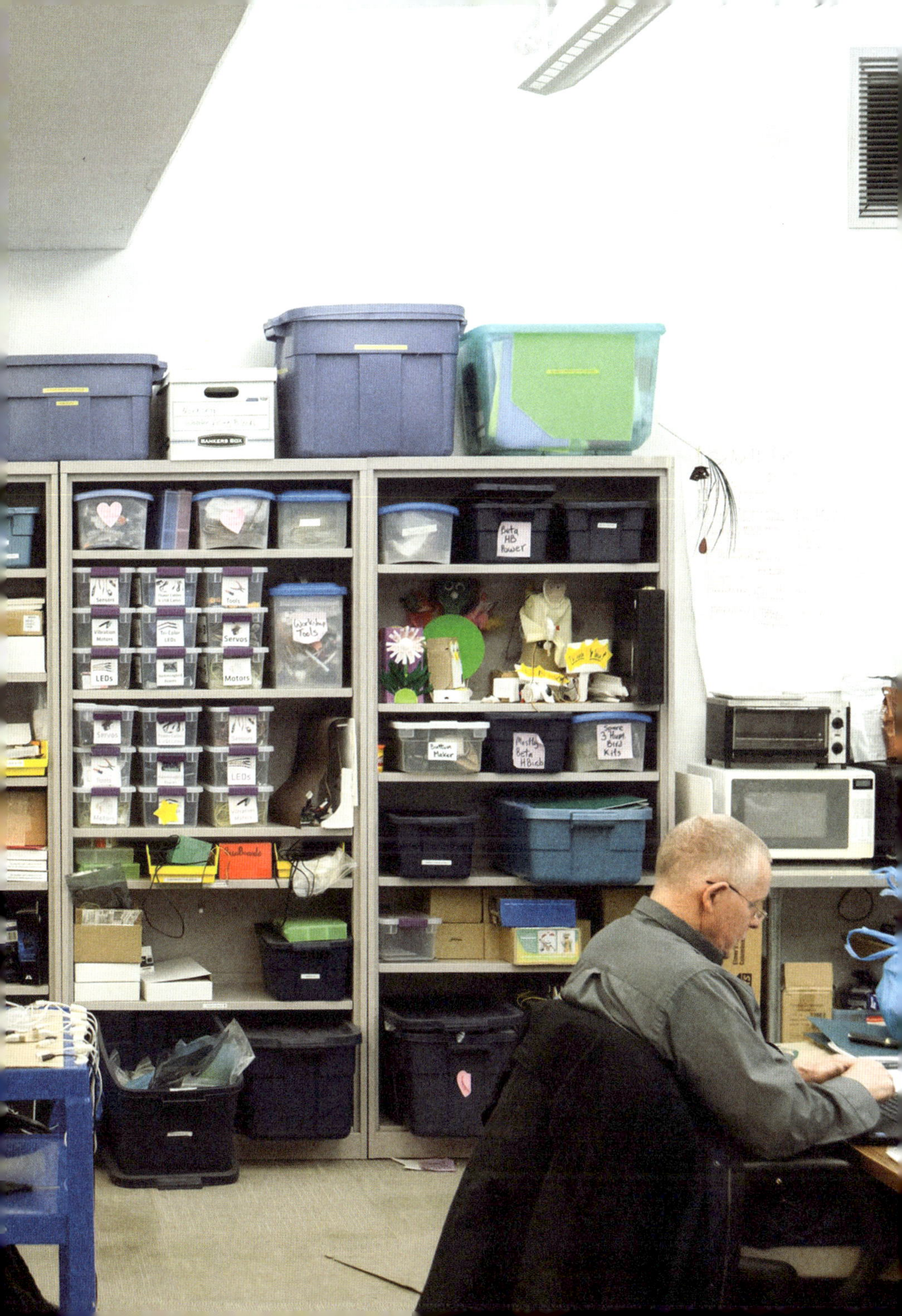

BANKERS BOX
Sensors
Tools
Vibration Motors
Tri-Color LEDs
Servos
LEDs
Motors
Servos
Sensors
LEDs
Motors
Workshop Tools
Beta HB Power
Button Maker
Mostly Beta HBirch
Spare 3 Hum Bird Kits

100

care deeply about how to solve the environmental problems in our world by using technology to empower local communities.



Thaddeus Popovich

I'm an engineer by training, so I understand the geekiness that can be there. The CREATE Lab team are not like that. For them, I coined the term "huggable engineers," which means their personality shows through. They were willing to do more than any of us expected. Randy once came to my home on a Sunday to hook up a Speck monitor for us, which measures particle size 2.5 micron and smaller. Randy tested it to make sure it would reach back into the server at Carnegie Mellon. I mean, that's tremendous. He was smiling the whole time and was chatting with us— like, "This is what I do." They kept saying that this work was being done by a collective "we." It wasn't "them" doing one thing and "us" doing another.

Leah Andrascik

And the difference in the air today is amazing. The kids can play outside and I don't have to worry about pollution spikes. Two summers ago, we caught the worst event I ever saw on the camera. I was outside with my kids, and there was raw coke gas pouring into the air. We were less than a thousand yards away, across the river. The changes now have lifted a huge weight off our shoulders.

*Andrea Polli*

*How do you adapt a project like this to future situations or scenarios, or how might another community apply what was learned and accomplished in a very specific context like Allegheny County?*

Yen-Chia Hsu

Each community has different characteristics, different goals. When we develop a system, we cannot just follow one method. Unlike a traditional computer science problem with a clear definition, the problems within a local community are hard to fully observe at first. It can be quite vague even. This is why we use an iterative design process to gradually find challenges and solve them step-by-step; through this process, we can eventually reach our goal.

Randy Sargent

We're also building on top of open source software. The software we make ourselves is in return open source. Everything that you see in the Breathe Cam or in Shenango Channel can in turn be built into other things. We have a visiting student researcher who is taking the toolbox and building something for refineries in the San Francisco Bay area. It's important in the context of hacking, right? We're part of the bigger effort to collaborate. We can do things standing on the shoulders of all the people before us, and hopefully we contribute back so other people can continue to build on top.

Note

[1] For more information, please see Yen-Chia Hsu, Paul Dille, Jennifer Cross, Beatrice Dias, Randy Sargent, and Illah Nourbakhsh, "Community-Empowered Air Quality Monitoring System," in *Proceedings of the 2017 CHI Conference on Human Factors in Computing Systems* (New York: ACM, 2017), 1607–19.

[2] An interactive map of the region from the *Pittsburgh Post-Gazette* identifies the percentages of deaths from heart disease, lung cancer, and respiratory illnesses in relation to the national average. "Mapping Mortality," accessed July 31, 2017, multimedia.post-gazette.com/MappingMortality/maps_mortality.

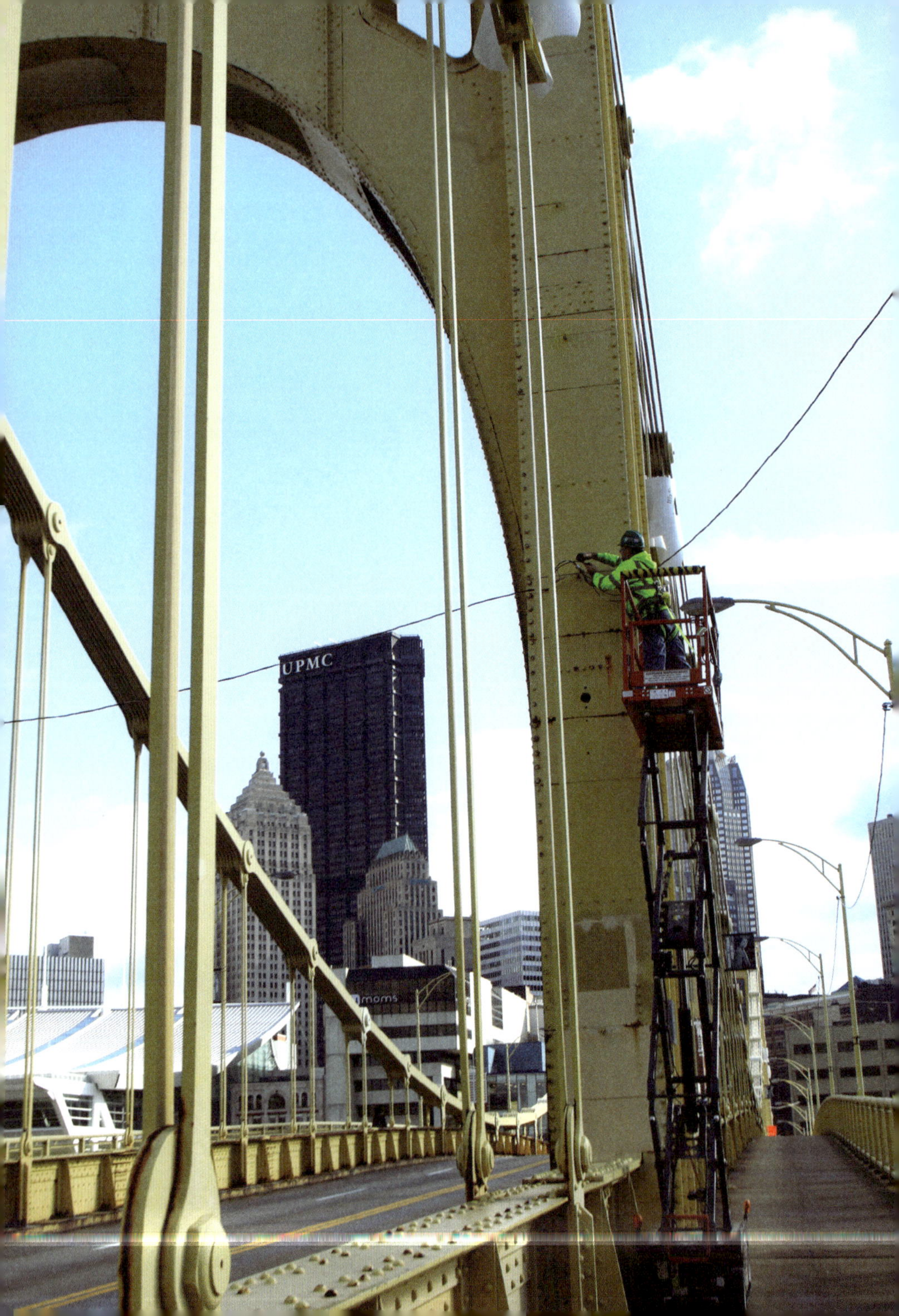
UPMC

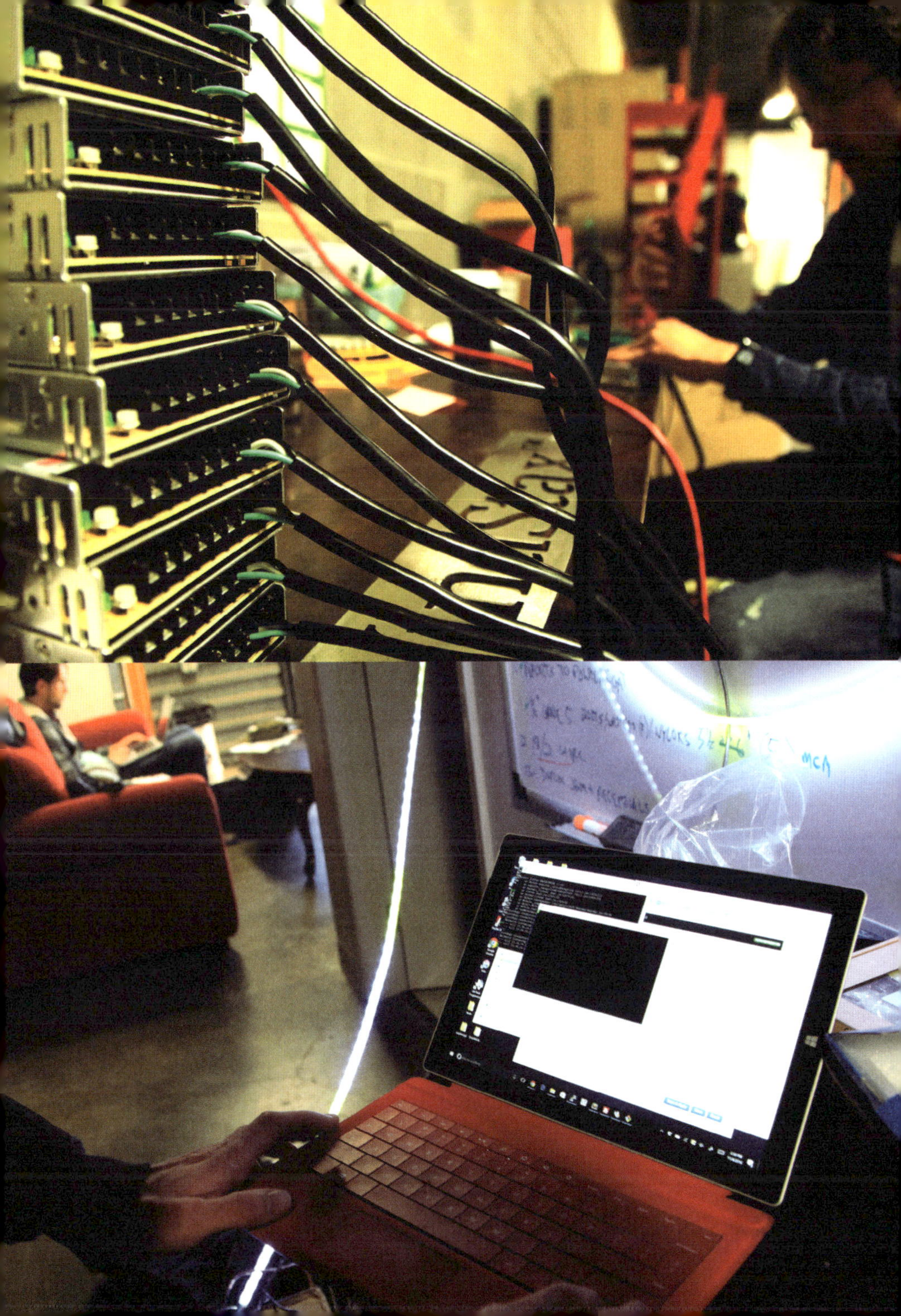

# Energy Flow

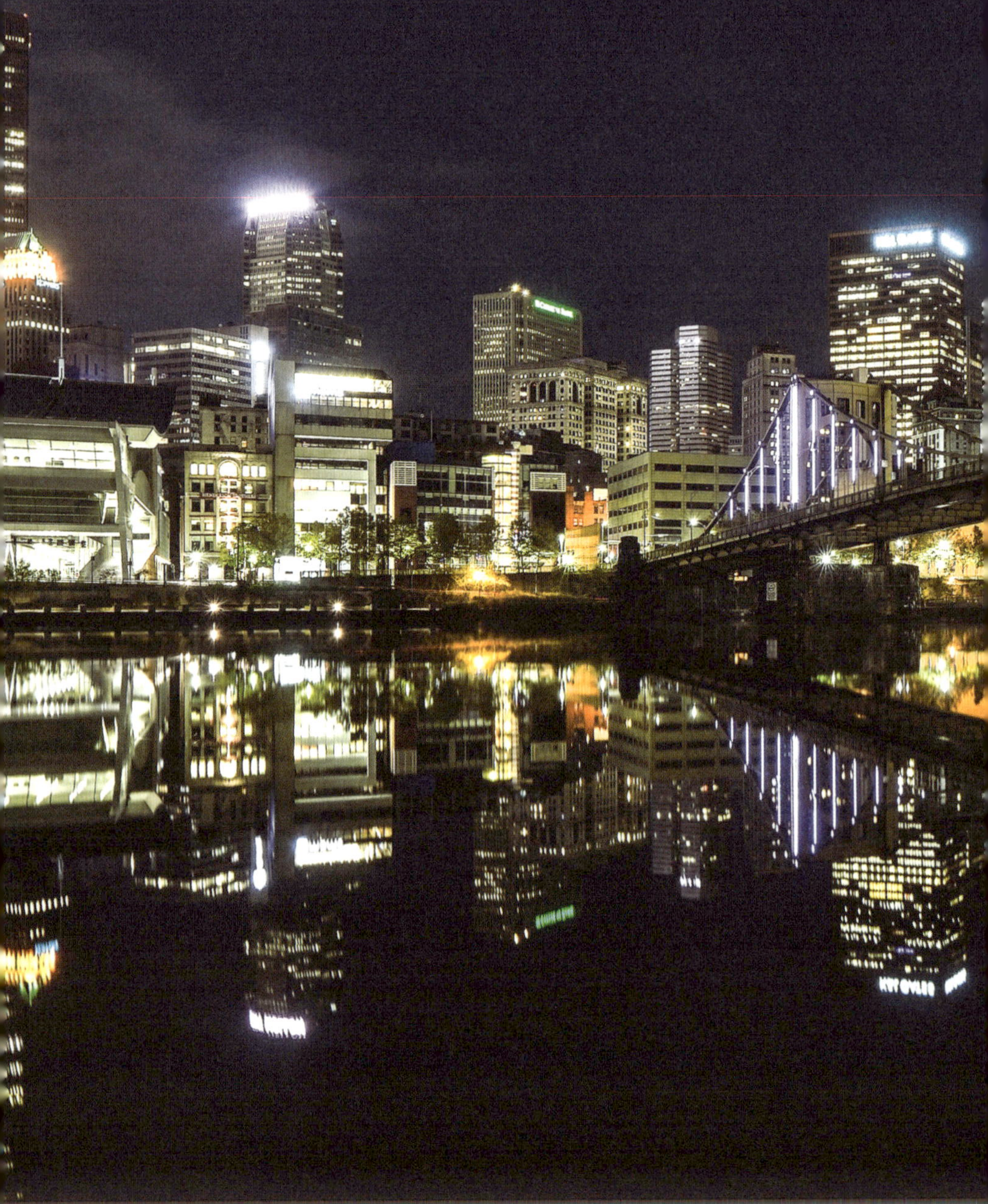

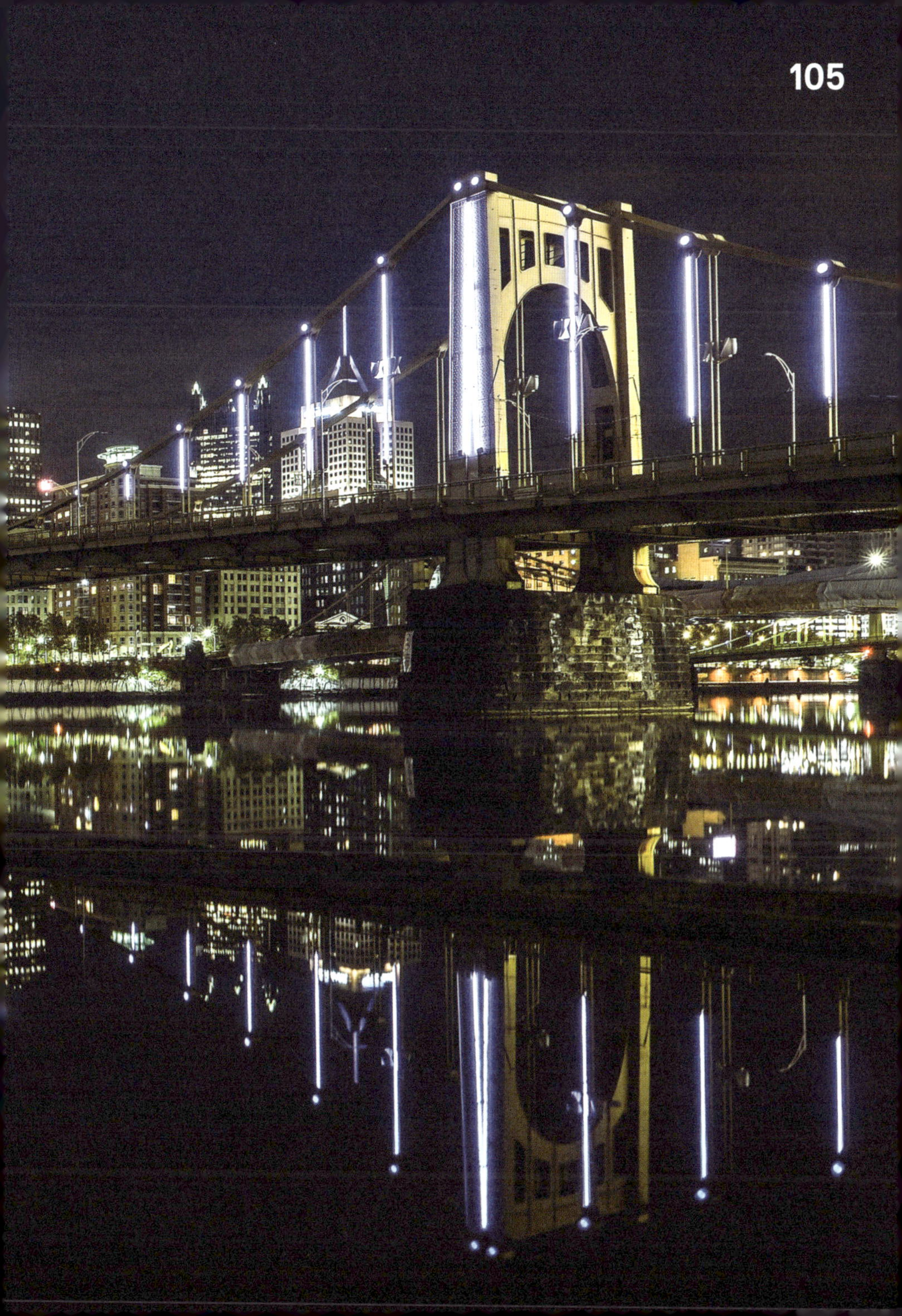

In the fall of 2001, I was living in a borough of New York City and working in midtown Manhattan. I walked or rode my bike over the Queensboro Bridge every morning, and I looked at the bridge from my apartment window every night.[1] Around that time, I had been working on some projects in collaboration with meteorologist Glenn Van Knowe. Glenn's company, MESO Inc., provides detailed weather prediction models to help determine the best placement and layout of wind farms. He told me, however, that the biggest obstacle to the installation of non-polluting wind energy was the public perception that wind farms are ugly—an eyesore on the landscape, or so many people seemed to think. While I was talking to him on the phone, I looked out my window and began to count the smokestacks around the Queensboro Bridge. I stopped at twenty. Belching their gray clouds into the air, these smokestacks were the ugliest things I could imagine, while to me wind turbines are beautiful in both aesthetics and function.

On September 11, I walked home early with thousands of others who had gone to work expecting just another day. The subways and other public transit had been temporarily suspended, and the Queensboro Bridge became our lifeline. Shoulder to shoulder, we made our way back home to our families. At some point later on—perhaps several months or a year—I noticed that the sparkling necklace lights that outlined the East River bridges' cables, which had ordinarily created a flowing line across the river, were suddenly dark at night. I learned that the necklace lights did not provide illumination to pedestrians or drivers on the bridge; they had been "merely" aesthetic, and the cost of the energy to light them had now become too expensive. I thought, what if renewable energy could actually enhance urban aesthetics as public art can? What if clean energy could not only improve the air we breathe, but increase our enjoyment of the city?

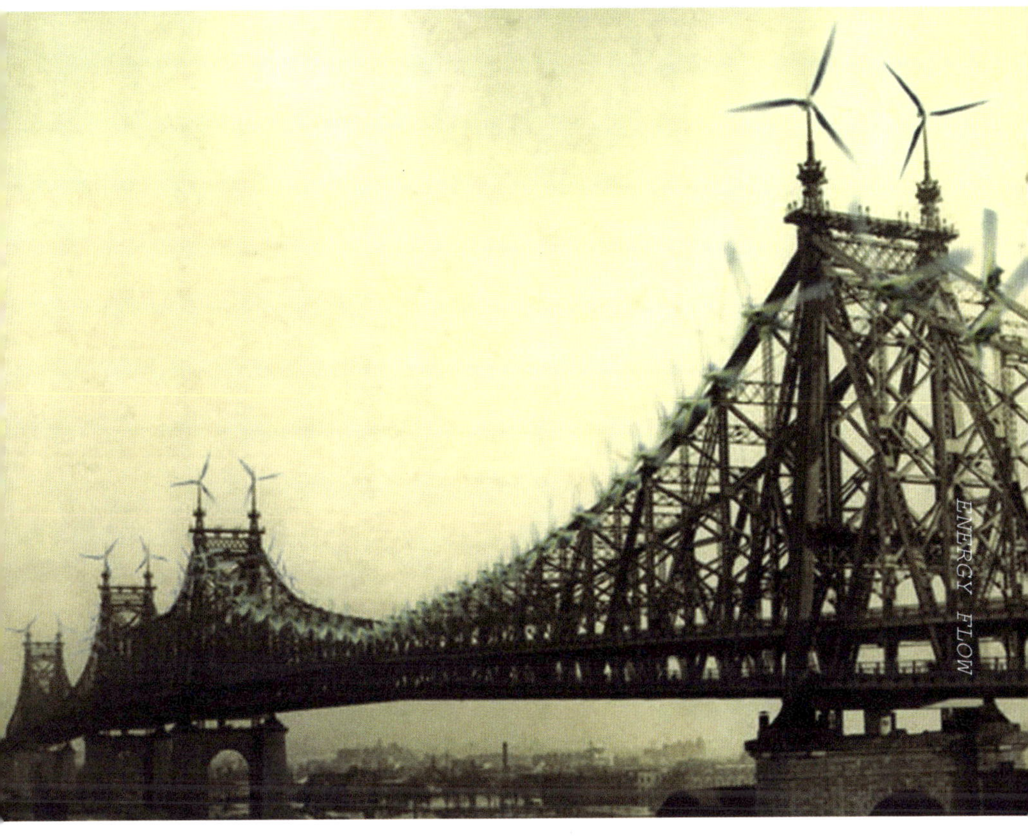


Andrea Polli, visualization of the
Queensbridge Wind Power Project, 2004

In order to address this problem, I developed a concept proposal to install wind turbines where there once were tall spires on the top of the Queensboro Bridge, and to use the power generated by the turbines to illuminate the necklace lights. I worked with an engineer to determine what we would need and how much energy we could create. We determined that the cost of installing

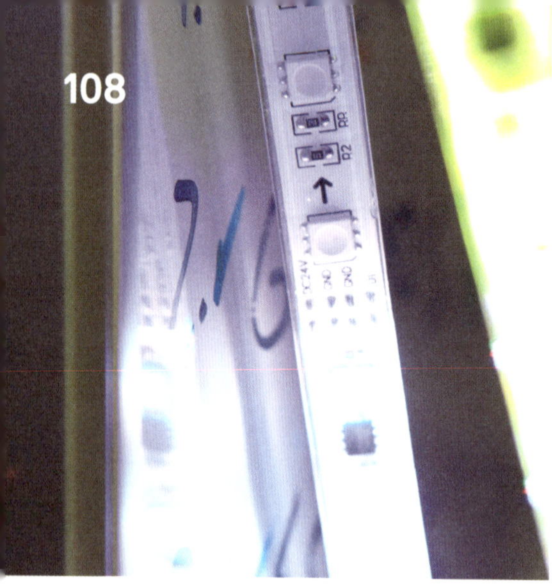



Left: **LED strips used by** *Energy Flow*

Below: **Chris Clavio at the WindStax warehouse**

Opposite page: **Installation of** *Energy Flow*, **2016**

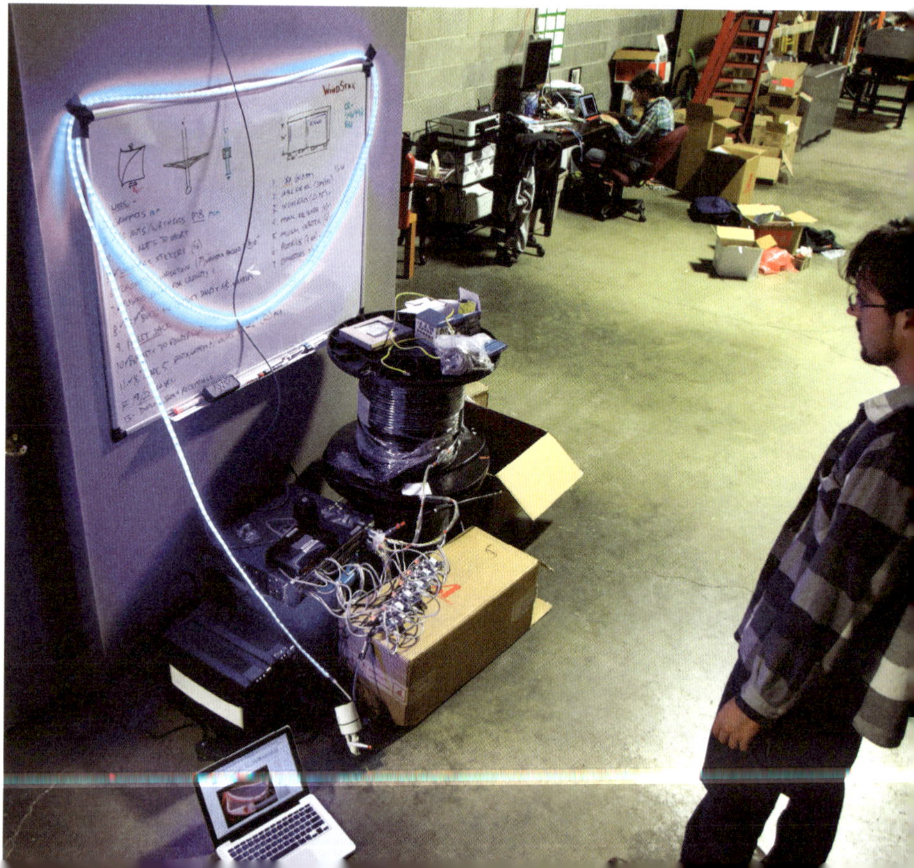

ANDREA POLLI

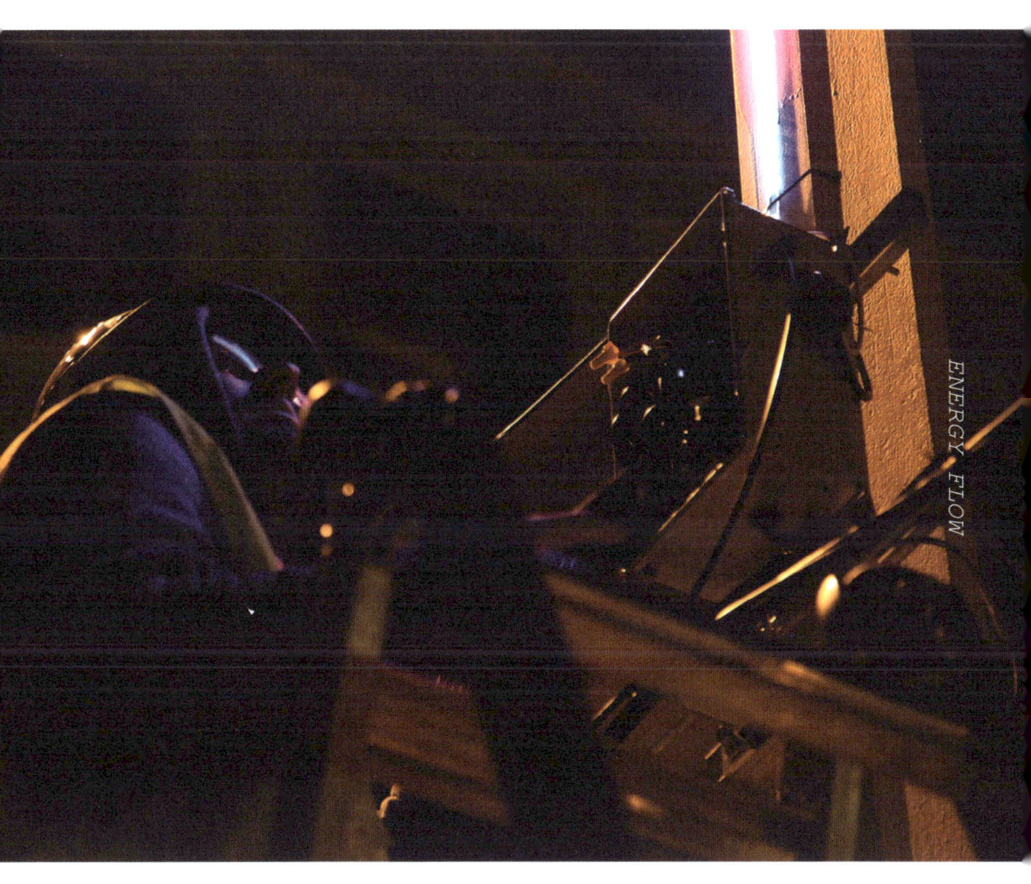
ENERGY FLOW

the system would be several million dollars, but that it would pay for itself with power generation in five years. While to me a five-year payback seemed phenomenal, I discovered that from the perspective of the power company, most power-generating projects were expected to have a two- or three-year payback maximum. Disheartened, I set the Queensbridge Wind Power Project aside and turned my attention to learning the tools used by engineers to create feasibility studies for wind and alternative energy systems. I began collecting data from professional weather stations and sharing this information with community and art centers across the US, Europe, South America, and Asia.

Fifteen years later, I was granted the opportunity to create a light-based, wind-powered artwork on the Rachel Carson/9th Street Bridge in Pittsburgh. Like the Queensboro Bridge and the East River bridges in New York, the "Three Sisters" bridges that span the Allegheny River in downtown Pittsburgh provide an important lifeline for the city's inhabitants. The 9th Street Bridge opened in 1926, a time between the two world wars when new technologies like radio and new art forms like jazz were transforming the country and promoting new visions for the future. We are in a similar moment today with the development of our distributed grid; while radio connected people at a distance with information and culture, our contemporary electrical grid connects energy generators with energy consumers. The "bridge" created by the grid can be a great equalizer, with small-scale wind and solar producers sharing power on the same network as a giant coal-fired power plant.

In creating *Energy Flow* on the Rachel Carson Bridge, I was fortunate to partner with the local Pittsburgh wind energy provider WindStax. CEO Ron

Gdovic had also been thinking about wind turbines on bridges for over fifteen years, and he had already done a feasibility study for wind power on the Allegheny bridges. For this project, WindStax designed beautiful, custom turbines that move slowly with a high amount of torque to not only efficiently generate power, but also be safe for birds. The safety of wildlife was a critical concern for us because the bridge is named for environmentalist Rachel Carson, a Pittsburgh native whose book *Silent Spring* (1962) was an important catalyst for the contemporary American environmental movement.

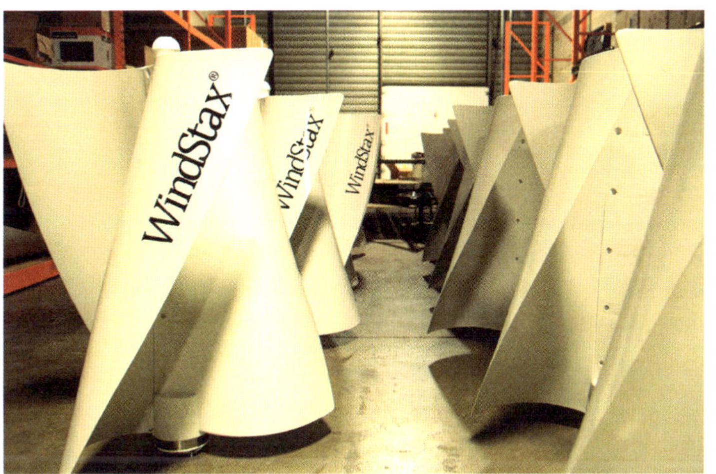


Custom WindStax turbines designed for *Energy Flow*

Ron and his WindStax team created an advanced energy management system combining wind energy and Duquesne Light utility power. *Energy Flow* uses sixteen 300-watt WindStax vertical axis turbines in clusters of four turbines, creating a nanogrid of small-scale, localized energy production. *Energy Flow* should produce approximately 10,800 kWh of wind energy annually— enough to power the average US household. In terms

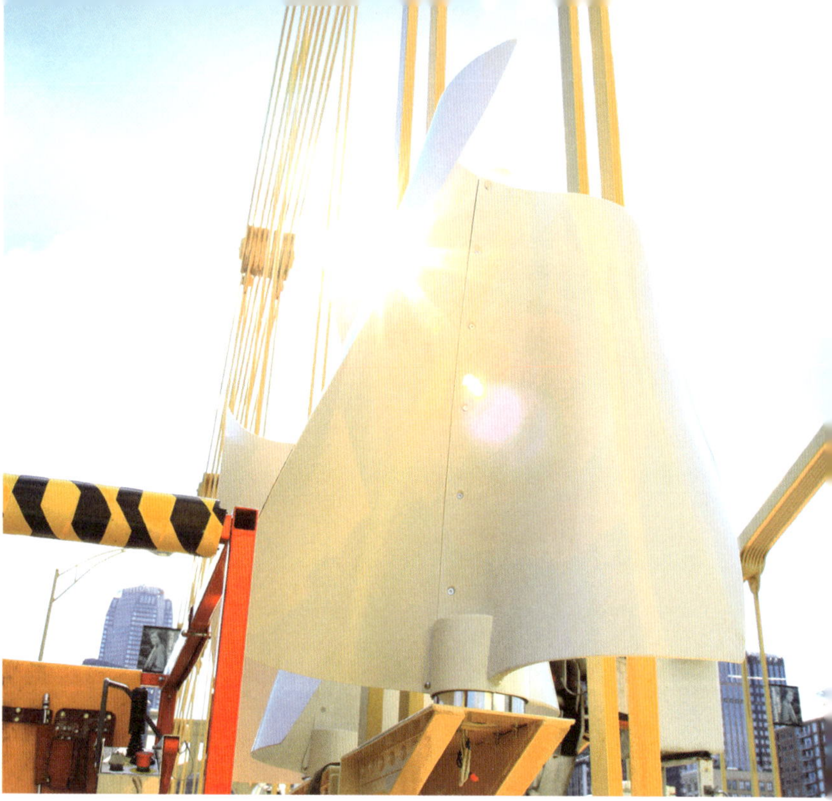

ANDREA POLLI

Installation of
*Energy Flow*, 2016

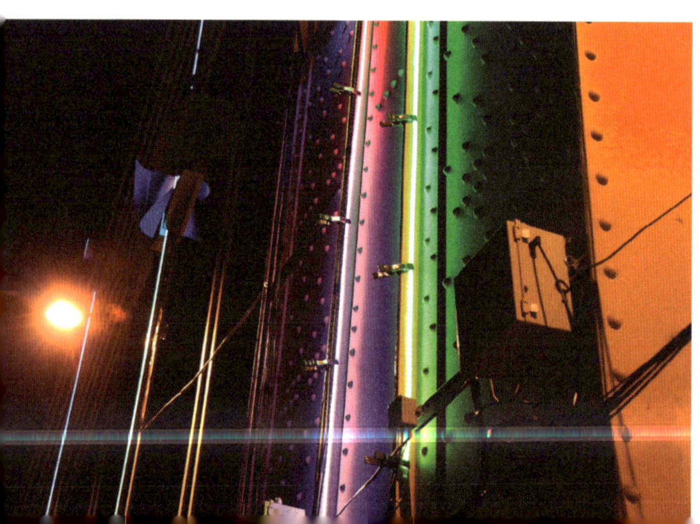

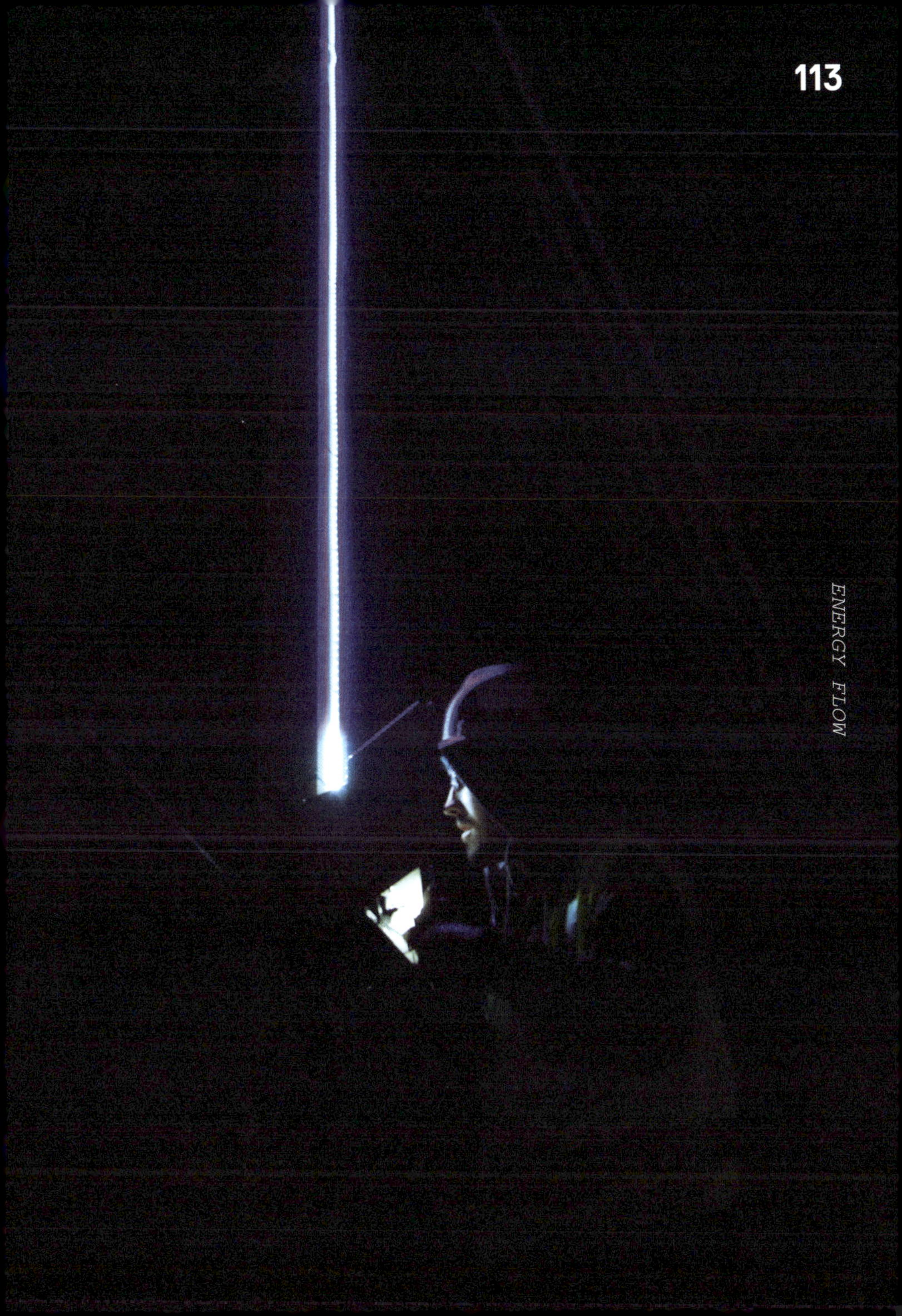

ENERGY FLOW

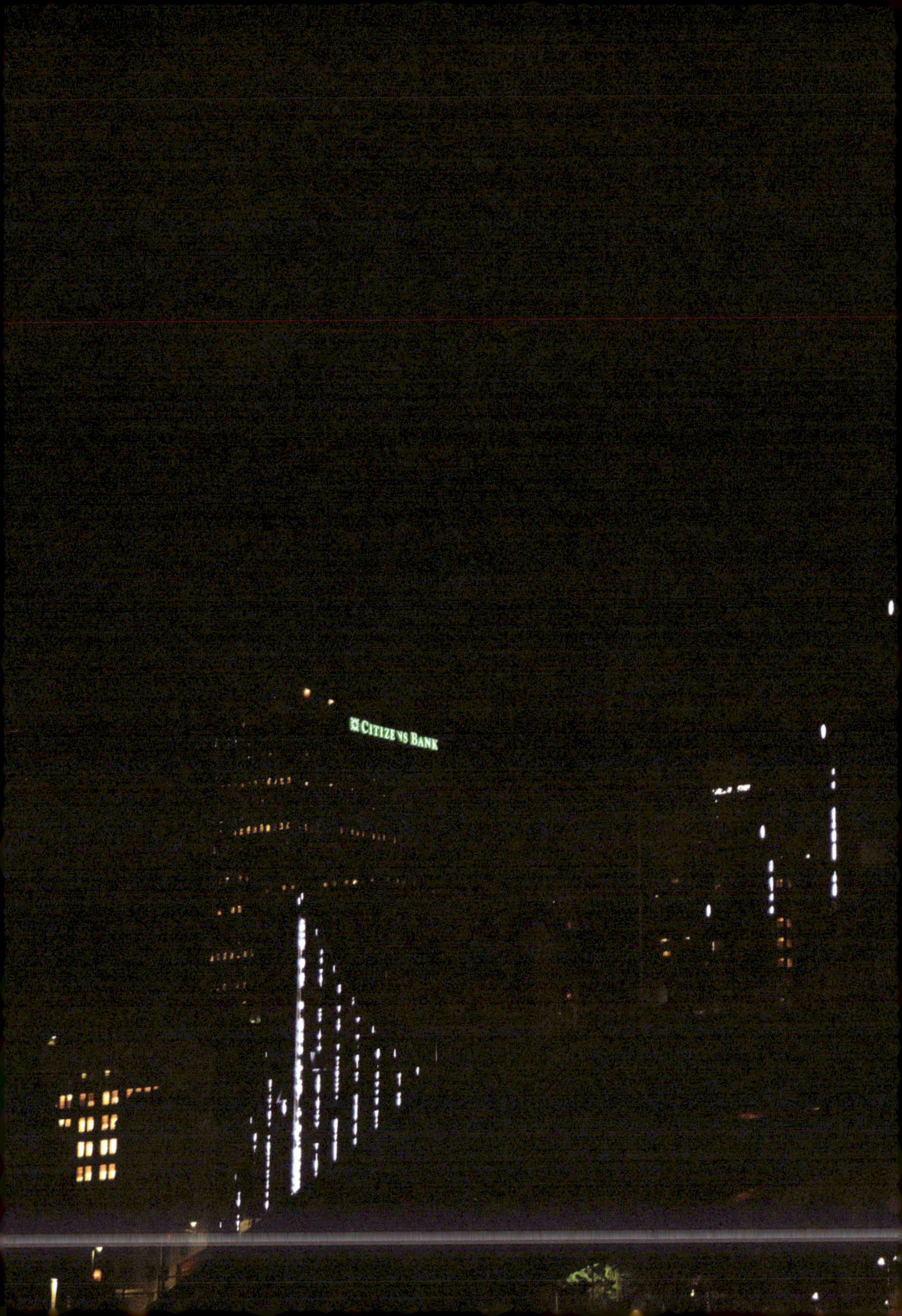
CITIZENS BANK

GATE
PT
E

of an annual reduction in carbon monoxide emissions, this is equivalent to taking 1.6 passenger vehicles off the road, eliminating 18,191 miles driven, or reducing 8.4 tons of carbon dioxide equivalent from the environment.

With the help of my lighting infrastructure designer, Chris Clavio of ClaviOn Unlimited, and visual designer and programmer Eric Geusz, we covered the span of the bridge with over 27,000 individually controllable LED lights that were capable of millions of color combinations. When the lighting display turns on, 24-volt direct current from the batteries is inverted to 120-volt alternating current to operate the lighting. The wind turbines continue to charge the batteries when the wind speed is above eight miles per hour. Should utility power be lost, the lighting will function for up to twelve hours, even with no wind.

Using wind and temperature data from a weather station on the bridge, the infrastructure that we created for the lighting system manages over fifty microcontroller computers to coordinate a series of animations and a real-time visualization of power potential. This not only allows viewers to see the invisible forces surrounding them at the moment, but also invites them to consider how energy could be generated from these and other phenomena. Through this, we were able to extend the basic concept outlines of the Queensbridge Wind Power Project proposal to an artwork that not only provides beauty to the city of Pittsburgh, but also conveys real-time information through a display of moving, colored light, turning the bridge into a compelling visual artwork that can be seen from many miles away. Evoking a rainbow—the visible product of an interaction between light and life-sustaining rain—the design of the lights links a naturally occurring environmental phenomenon with a computer-generated representation. *Energy Flow*

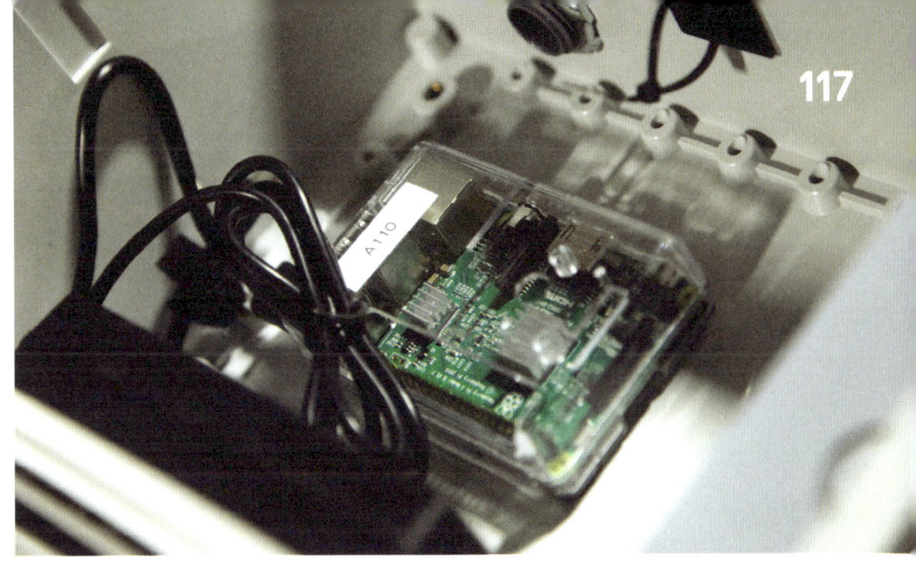

Above: **One of fifty-two raspberry Pi microcontrollers used for _Energy Flow_**

Below: **From left to right: Andrea Polli, Ron Gdovic, Chris Clavio, and Mark Goyke at the Windstax warehouse**

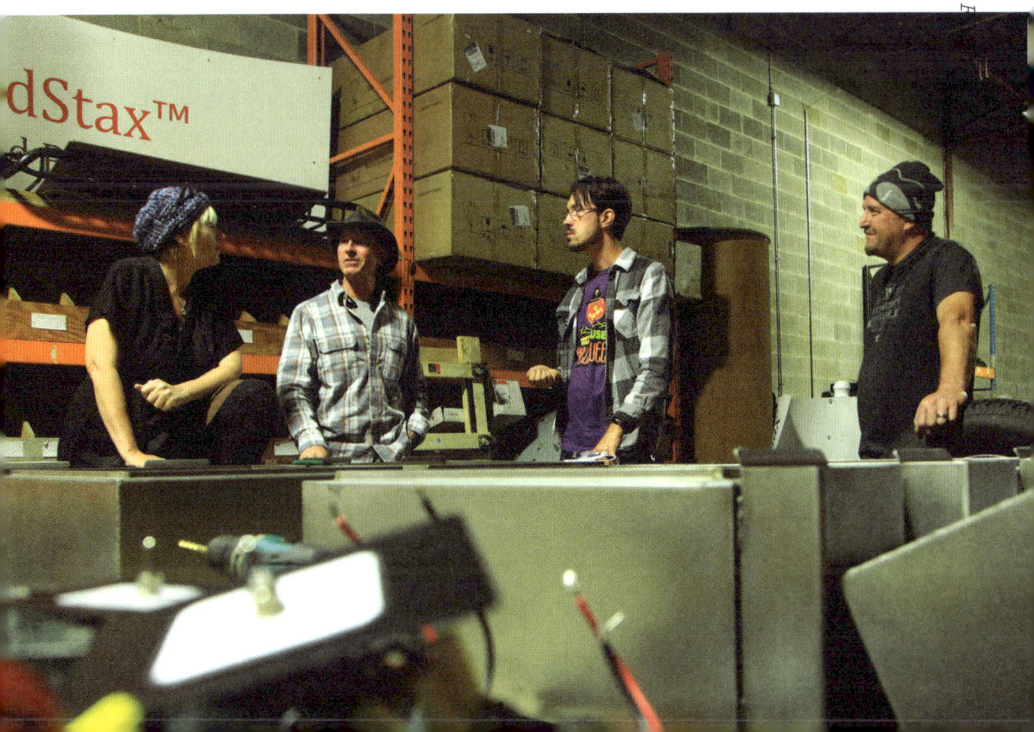

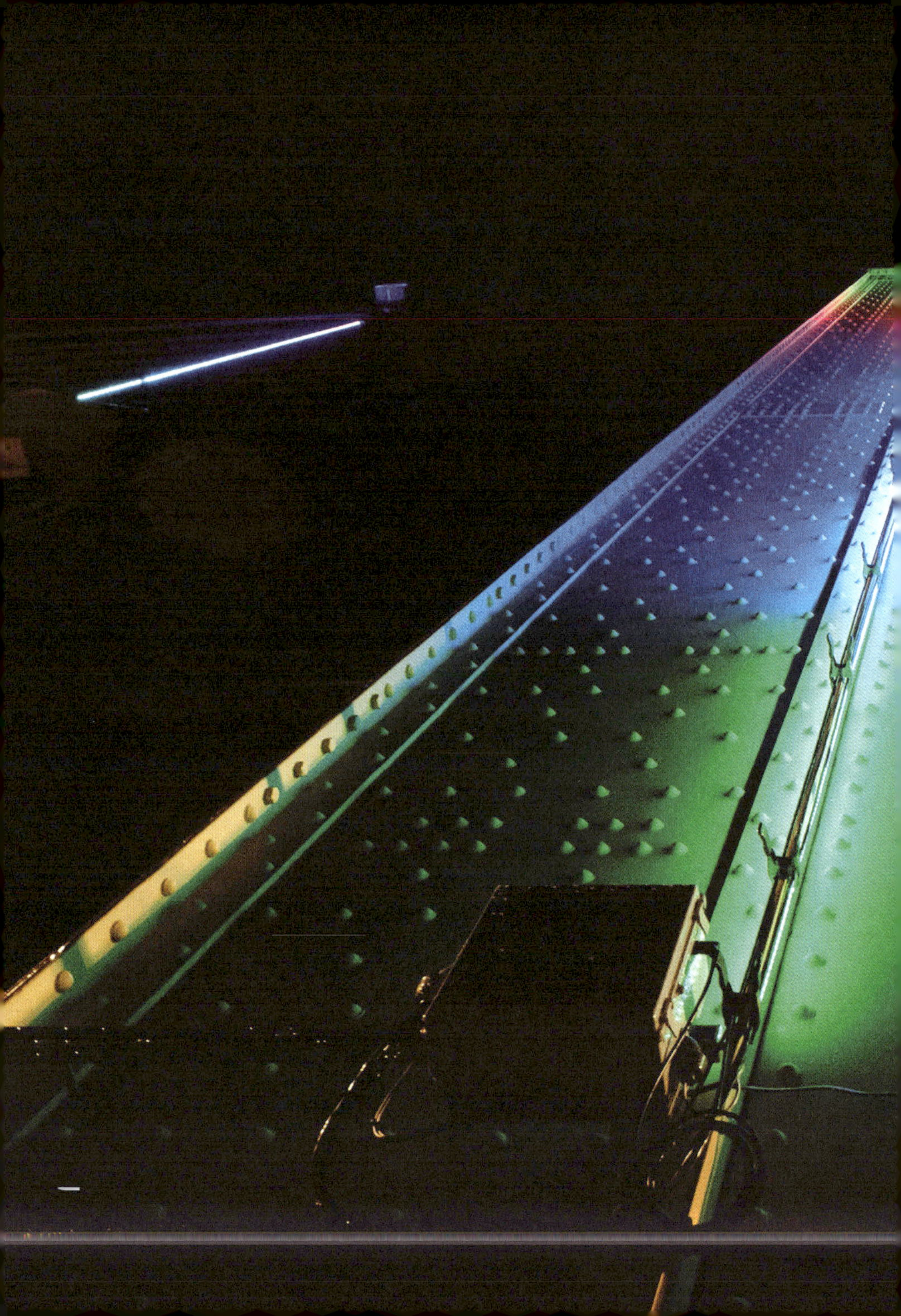

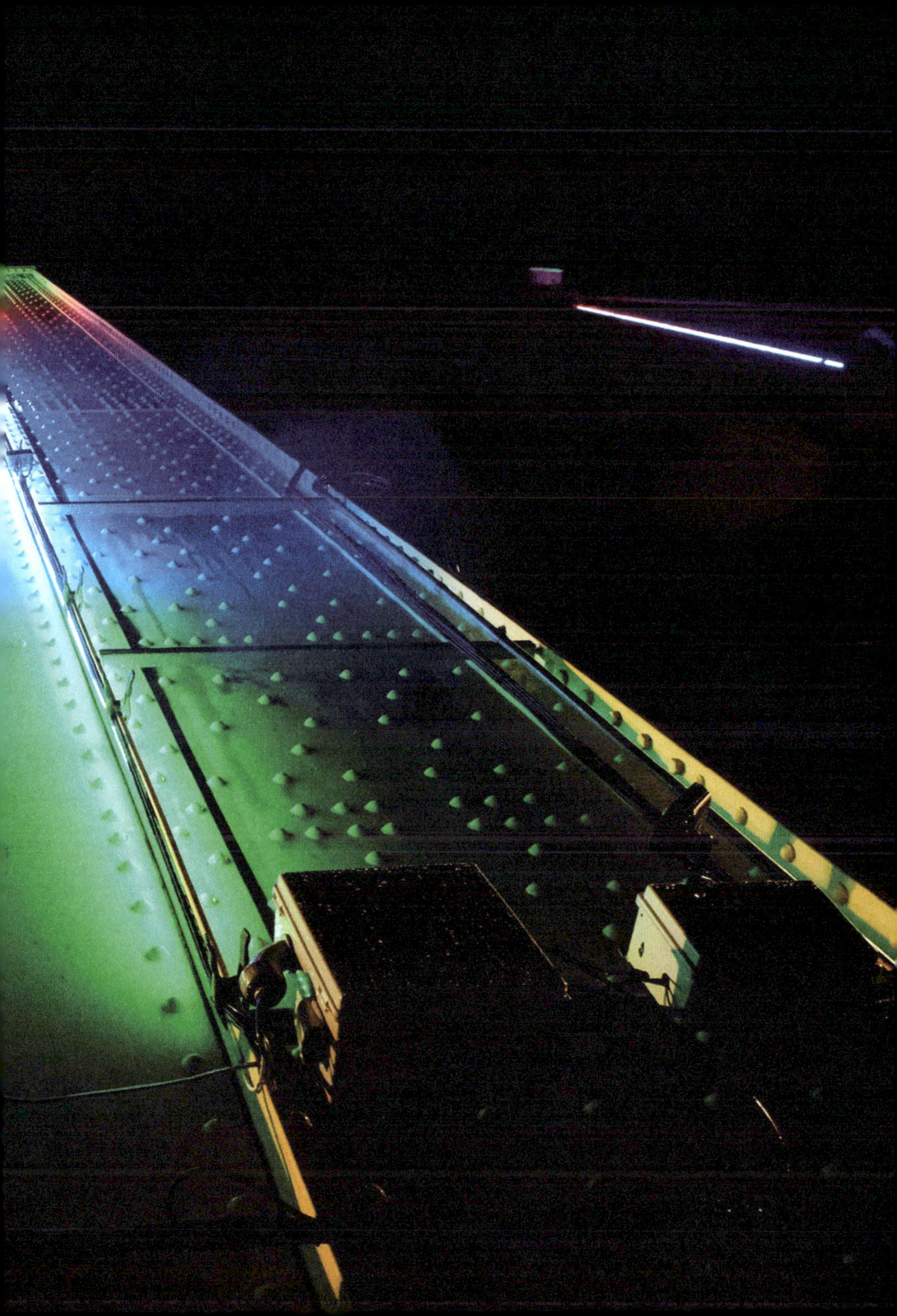

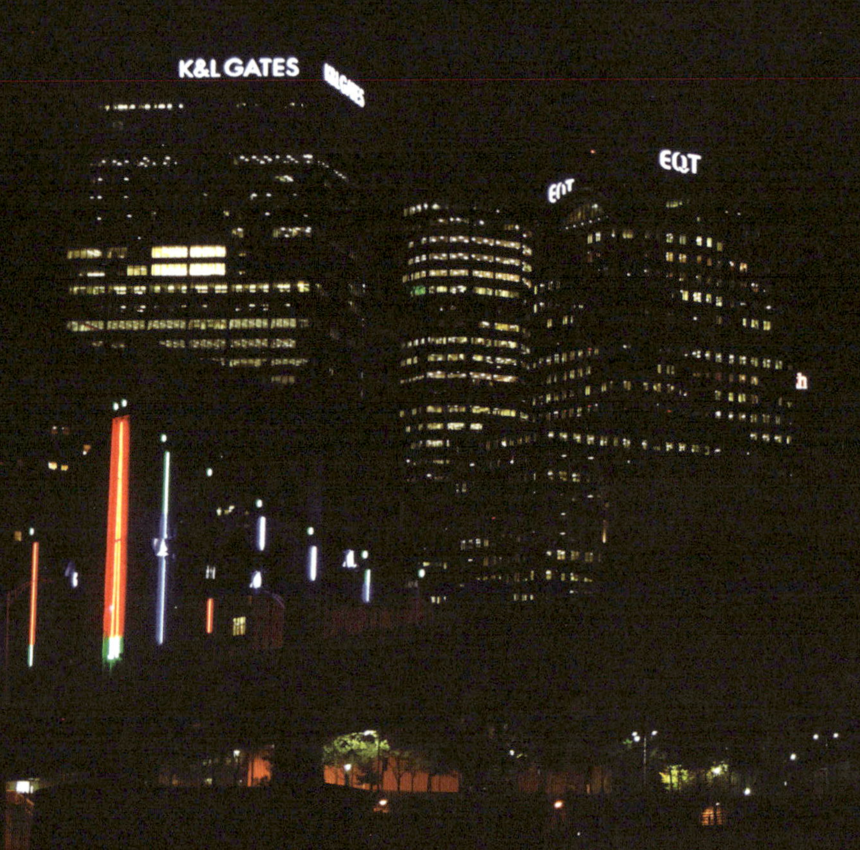
K&L GATES
EQT
EQT

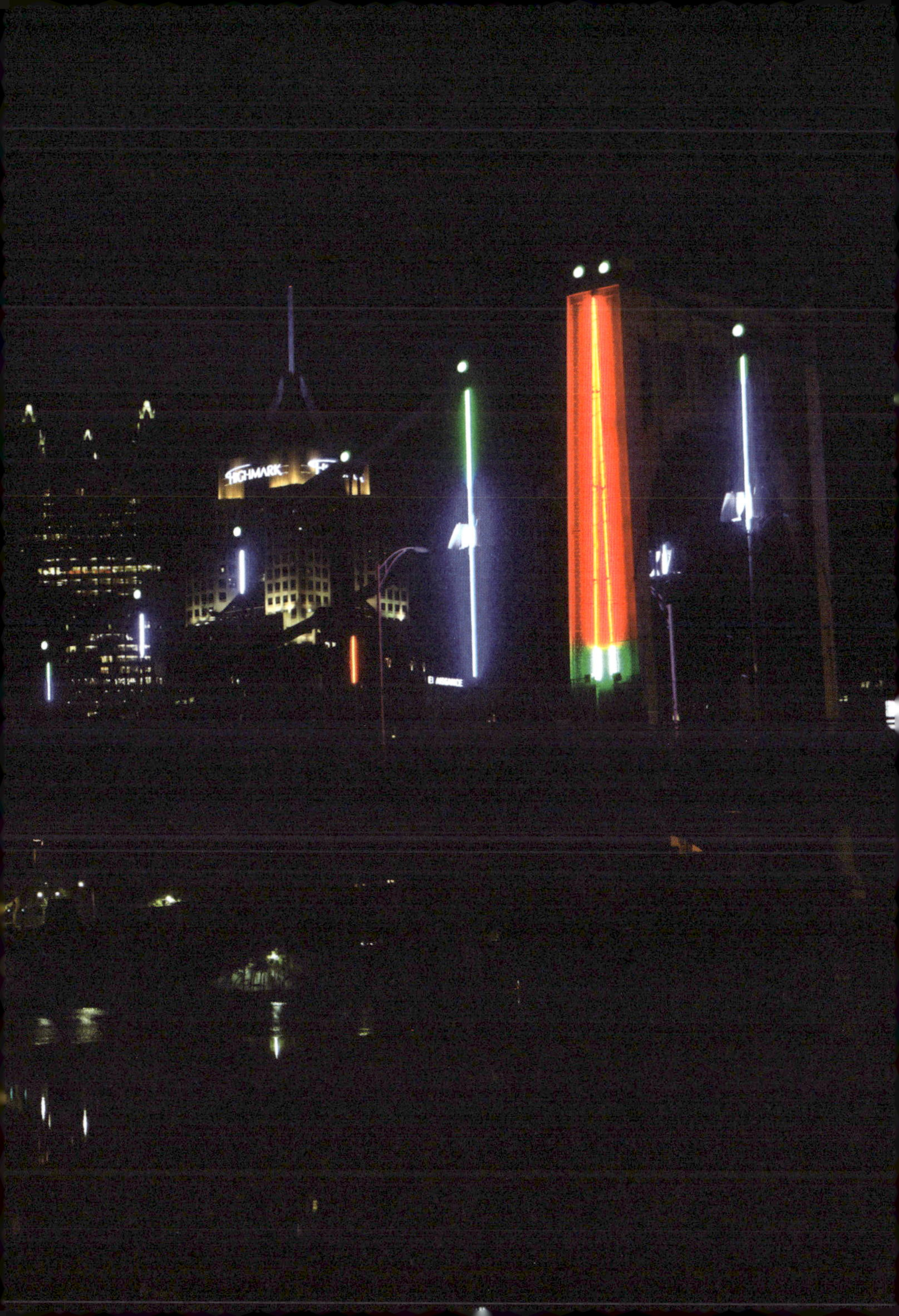
HIGHMARK

ANDREA POLLI

offers a glimpse into the future of smart grid technology, blending traditional and alternative energy sources to create both a reliable source of energy and real-time visual information.

At a Carnegie Museum of Art workshop in downtown Pittsburgh, I convened people from throughout the city to discuss how data visualization and public art can motivate conversations about environmental sustainability and environmental justice. Using *Energy Flow* as a case study, I guided participants through sensing and visualization strategies to imagine inventive, aesthetic, and informative lighting design concepts for the bridge. Before the workshop concluded, we walked down to the Rachel Carson Bridge to see *Energy Flow* up close and better understand the connections between artistic decisions and aesthetic impact. Participants then made and used simple LED "throwies"—colored LED lights attached to magnets—to design their own bridge lighting on a silhouette image of the bridge.

*Energy Flow* has become a source of pride for Pittsburgh residents, and our team's ability to update the colors and animations in real time using a secure smartphone interface has allowed the city to quickly respond and voice its environmental and community values on an urban-scale platform.

Note

[1] Completed in 1909, The Queensboro Bridge spans the East River in New York City. It is alternately known as the 59th Street Bridge, Queensbridge, and the Queens Borough Bridge.

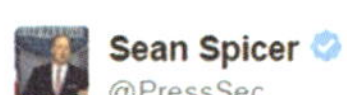

**Sean Spicer** ✓
@PressSec

**Follow**

.@POTUS "I was elected by voters of Pittsburgh, not Paris. I promised I wld exit or renegotiate any deal which fails to serve US interests"

12:54 PM - 1 Jun 2017

↩ ⇄ 5,970 ♥ 18,162 ℹ

**bill peduto** ✓
@billpeduto

**Follow**

As the Mayor of Pittsburgh, I can assure you that we will follow the guidelines of the Paris Agreement for our people, our economy & future. twitter.com/presssec/statu…

1:03 PM - 1 Jun 2017

↩ ⇄ 121,433 ♥ 248,298 ℹ

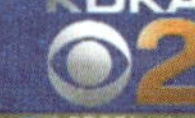


ENERGY FLOW

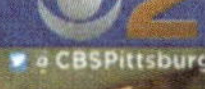

**KDKA** ✓
@CBSPittsburgh

Some #Pittsburgh landmarks are glowing green tonight in support of the #ParisAgreement -- cbsloc.al/2s3jzO6

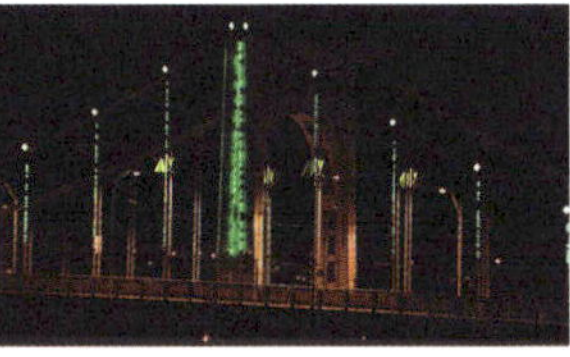

6/2/17, 10:34 PM

In early June 2017, *Energy Flow* was illuminated in green to signal support for the Paris Climate Accords

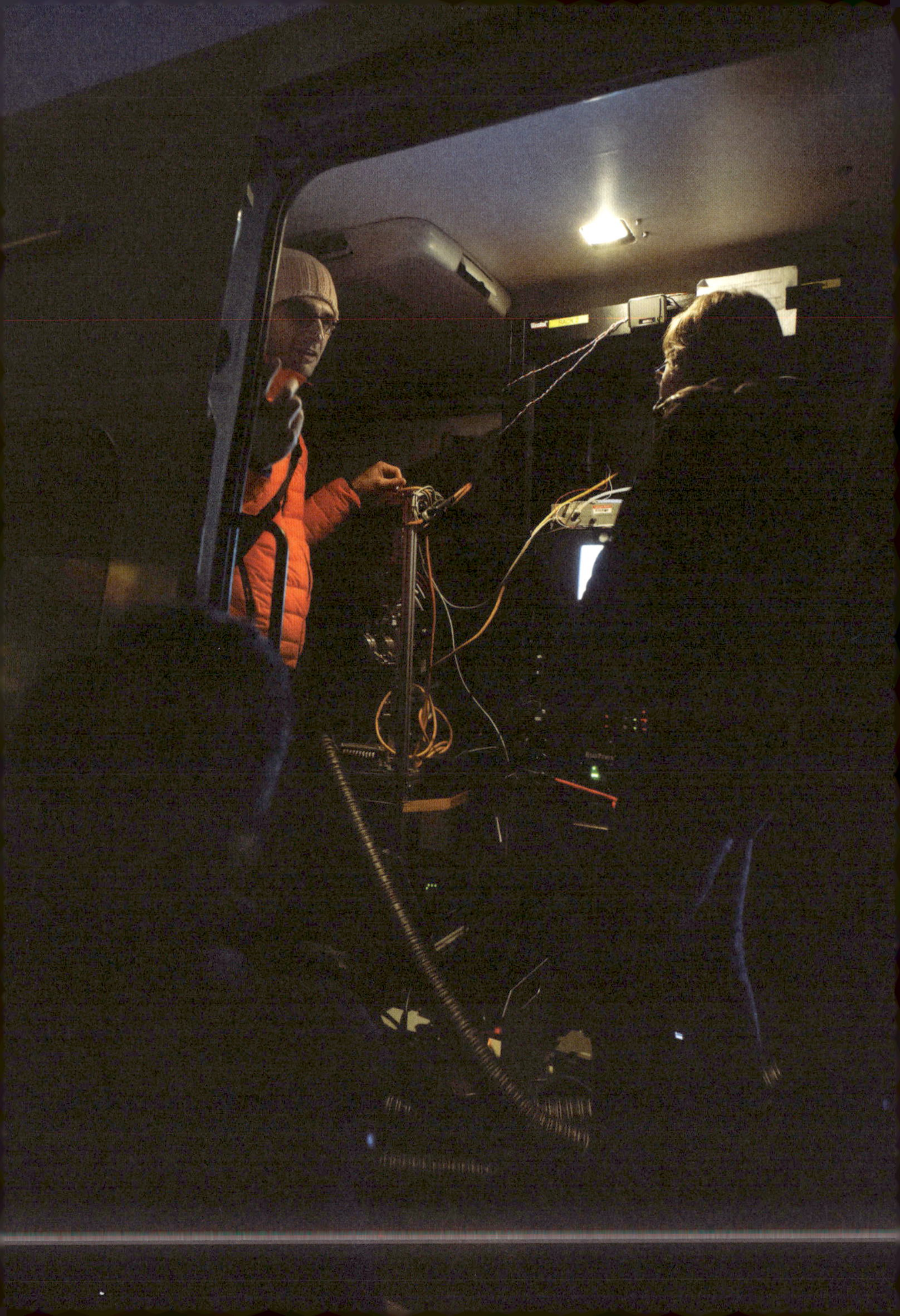

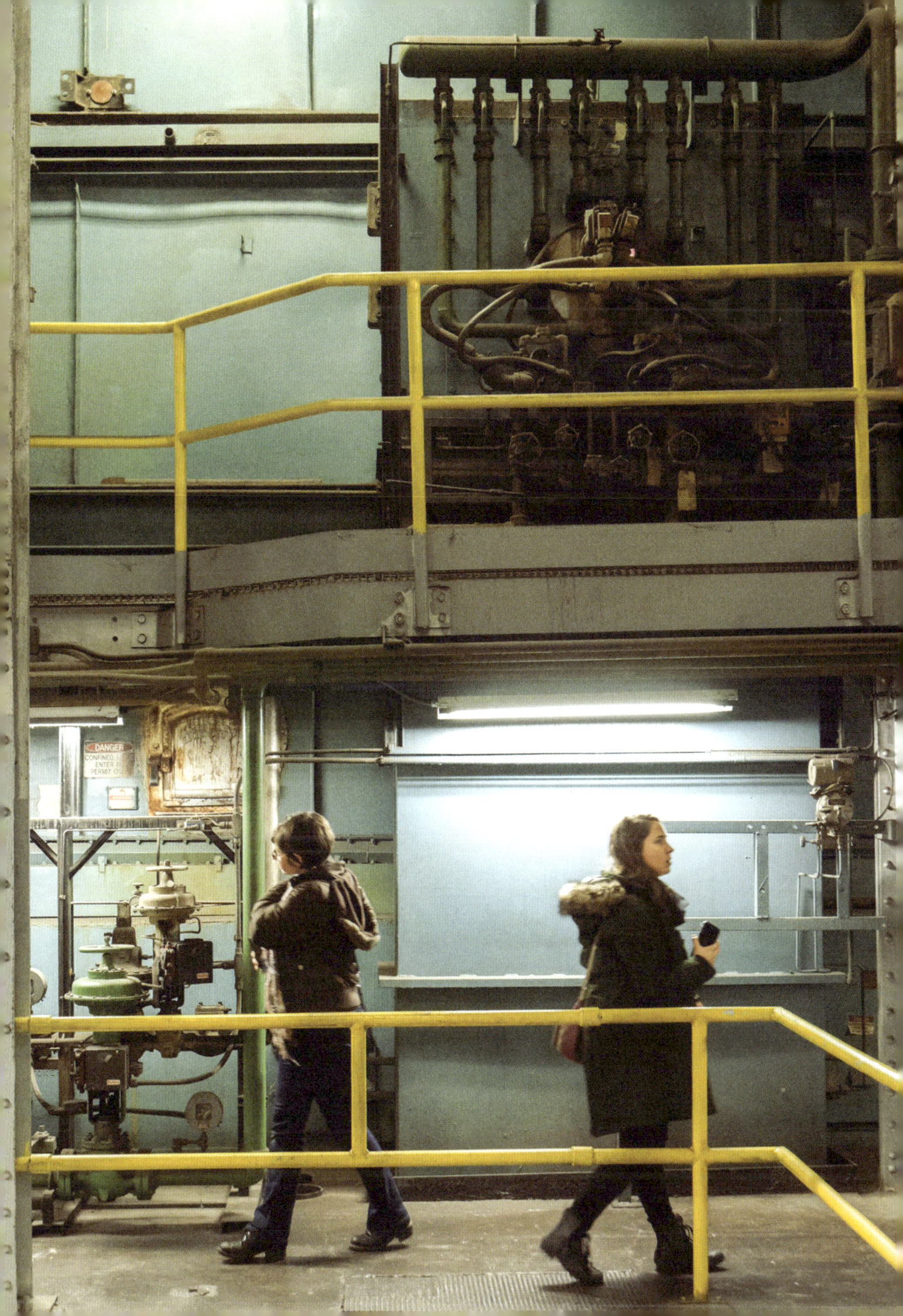

# The Cloud Factory: Workshops

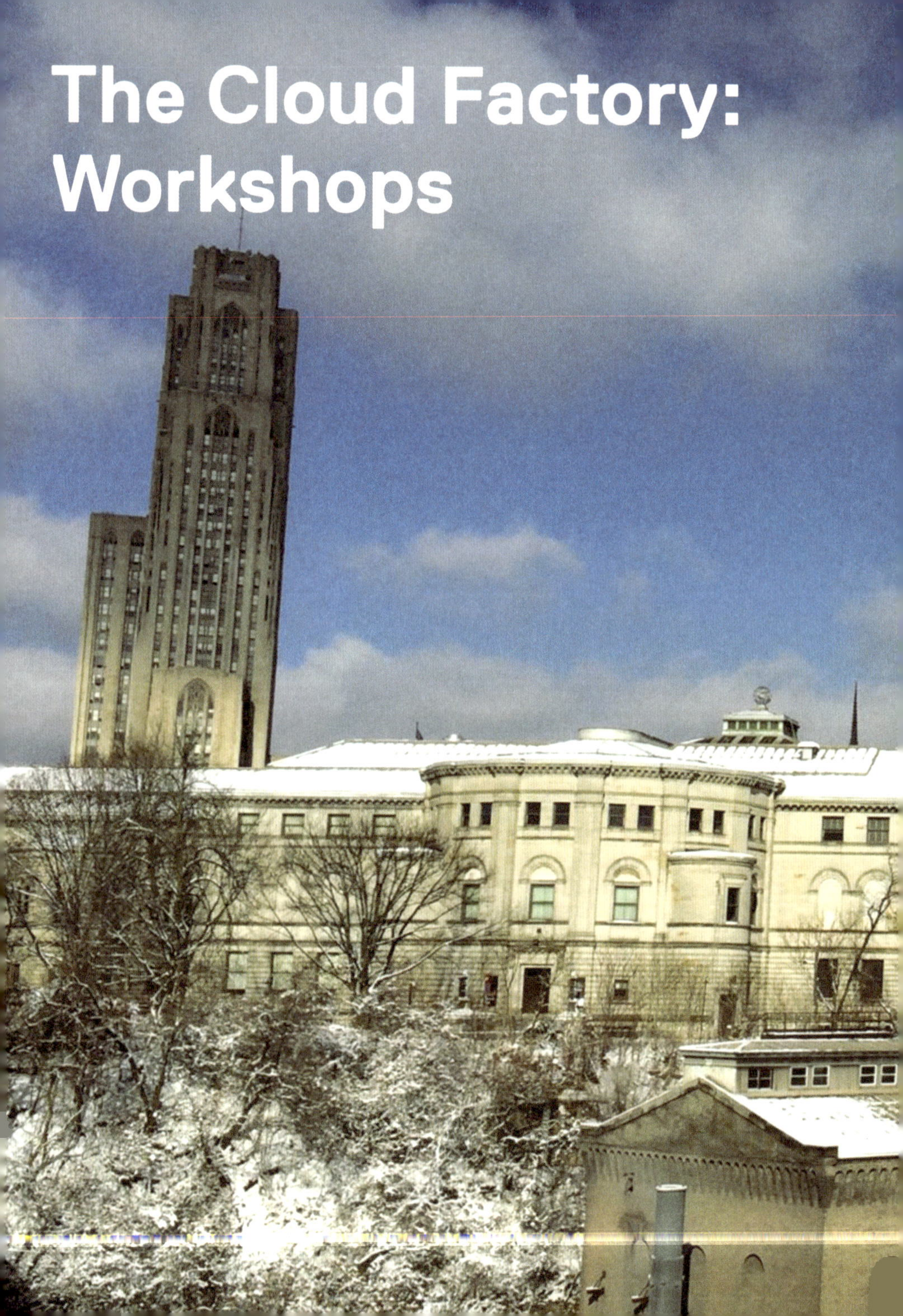

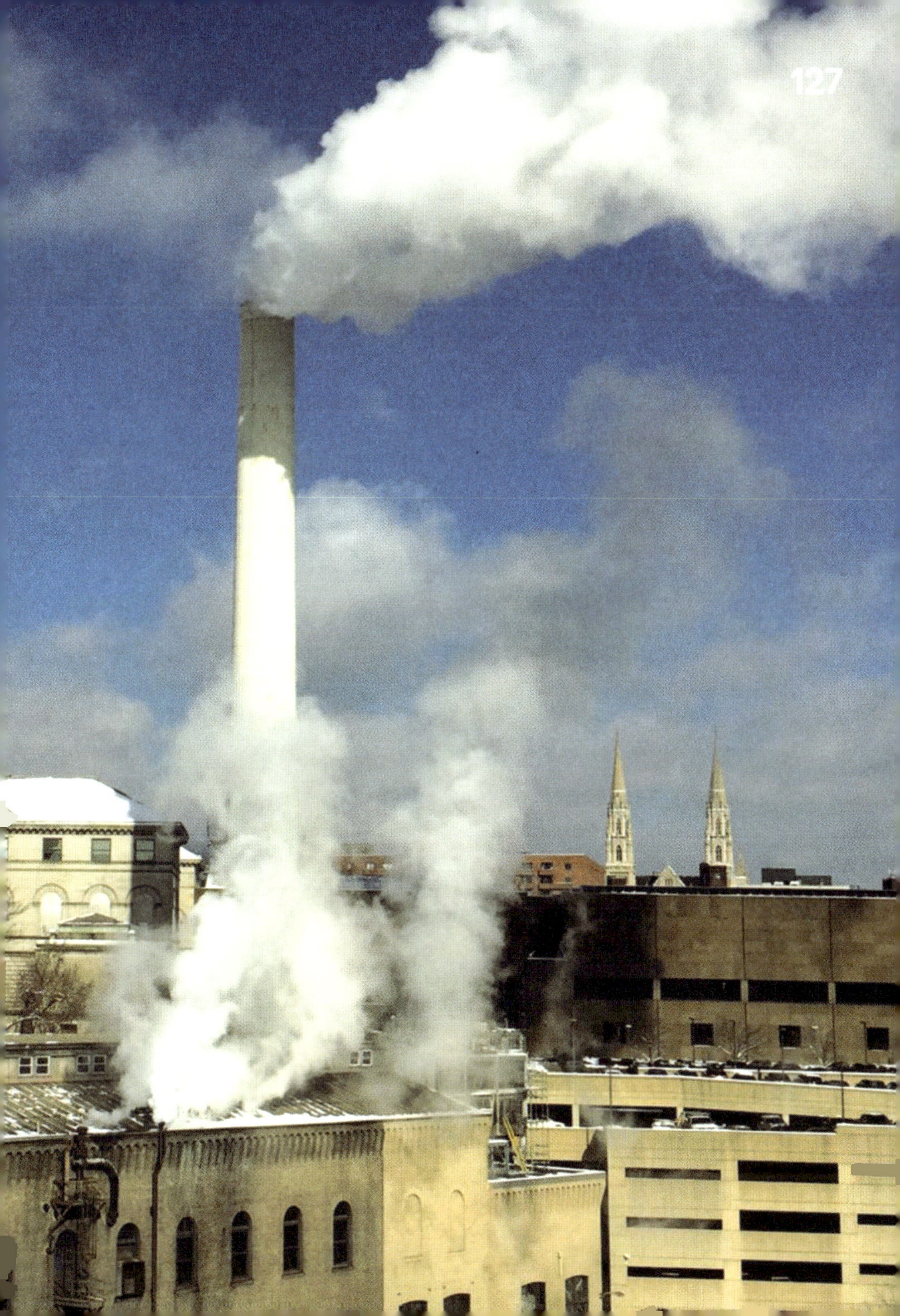

You enter the Grand Staircase of Carnegie Museums of Art and Natural History at the lowest level and are greeted by softly rendered images of laborers—a mural of workers shoveling and moving coal from railcars to furnaces. Painted smoke rises and twists from those furnaces, leading you up the stairs towards the skylight. As you ascend, the dark and deeply human images of the workers give way to a lighter and more ethereal scene. Here, angels emerge from the luminous pink and gray smoke. To an early twentieth-century observer, this mural was most likely seen as a celebration of the industrial future represented by Andrew Carnegie, who was said to be depicted by artist John White Alexander as a medieval knight. The pride of the workers, the economic boom that steel and coal created for Pittsburgh, and the enlightenment achieved through the museum's collection are all evident.

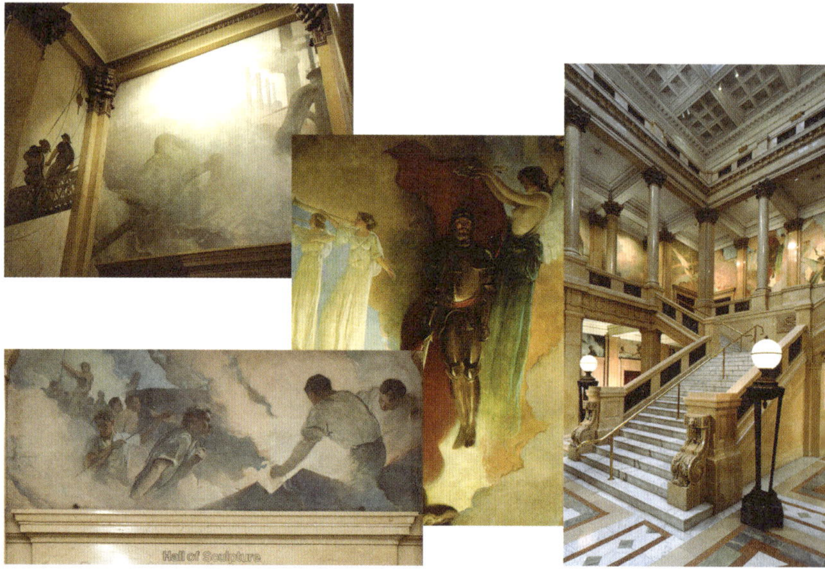


Details of John White Alexander,
*The Crowning of Labor*, 1907

But on the second floor, in a corner, there is a panel with red smoke that appears much darker than that of the angelic pink and gray. From the billowing red clouds, you see eyes expressing pain and anger, as well as what might be the horns of a demon. Do these eyes represent the souls of the workers below, who died from their labors? Are these the eyes of devils signaling the uncertain path of industry? A few panels away, one finds reprieve in another view of beautiful, ethereal angels. But you notice a tiny aberration that appears no larger than a playing card—a dark rectangle out of place on the otherwise pristine panel. You learn that this dark square was left by a team of conservators who cleaned and restored the mural in 1995. Although Alexander had added a protective layer of wax to the mural, soot and grime darkened the surface over time to the point of near invisibility. The conservators decided to leave a few untouched patches on each level as a nod to Pittsburgh's coal-fired history.

You walk back down and head towards the parking lot of the museum, stopping to admire the interactive art installations on the first floor and the colorful Sol Lewitt wall drawing that faces the windowed courtyard. Then, as you look out, you see it. The tall white smokestack of the Cloud Factory, also known as the Bellefield Boiler Plant—the most likely source of the particulate pollution that caused Alexander's *The Crowning of Labor* mural to darken so dramatically over the years. Built to provide steam heat to the museum in 1907—the same year Alexander began painting—the boiler now pumps heat to most of the major buildings in Pittsburgh's Oakland neighborhood.

The Bellefield Boiler burned coal for over one hundred years before it finally transitioned to natural gas in 2009. During its century of coal burning, the plant

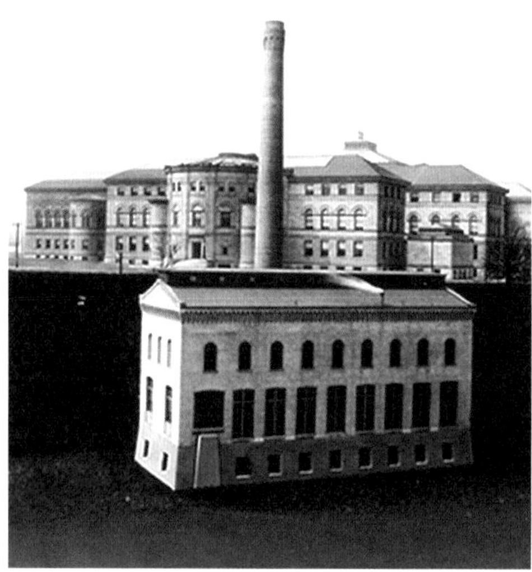

The Bellefield
Boiler,
ca. 1907

could consume up to a seventy-ton hopper car of coal
per day. The contemporary move to natural gas was
triggered in part by a series of air-quality violations.
In 2006, after the plant exceeded county air pollution
limits for particulates and sulfur dioxide, the owners (a
co-op of heating customers including the University of
Pittsburgh and their Medical Center, Carnegie Mellon
University, Carnegie Museums of Pittsburgh, Carnegie
Library of Pittsburgh, the City of Pittsburgh, and
Pittsburgh Public Schools) paid a large fine and agreed
to use a cleaner fuel mixture of coal and natural gas.
Then in October 2008, the plant was cited by the health
department for excessive visible emissions and made the
massive transition to all gas fuel, which was estimated to
reduce sulfur dioxide emissions by 99 percent (equivalent
to 700 tons per year) and particulate emissions by
76 percent (170 tons per year). Today there is talk
of the boiler becoming a "co-generation" plant, which
means that any excess heat that is generated would be

converted to electrical power, creating an efficiency gain that would become part of the electricity grid.

The boiler has also played a role in Pittsburgh's cultural history. In his 1988 novel *The Mysteries of Pittsburgh*, Michael Chabon referred to it as "the Cloud Factory," committing to print a nickname that may already have been in use colloquially. Chabon's description evokes the ethereal beauty of Alexander's mural: "When you walk across the Schenley Park bridge, there, from the park into Oakland, you pass above the Cloud Factory. What does it do? we used to wonder. Why do these great clouds, perfectly white and clean, white as new baseballs, come out of that building by the tracks?"[1] As a longtime advocate of renewable energy, however, and while working on a project with the museum about light and environmental sustainability, I found it challenging to see a smokestack as culturally significant, let alone beautiful. To me, most utilities are invisible, tucked away in a far corner of a city, intentionally out of sight. Alternately, smokestacks are so ubiquitous that I have learned to ignore them, like the 60-cycle hum of electricity that over time you just can't hear. Maybe the Cloud Factory would become invisible to me like this, but to see it for the first time was shocking— a giant smokestack almost literally on the grounds of the museum. Could such a structure become a platform for public works of art?

I wanted to see how native Pittsburghers saw the Cloud Factory, so I worked with the museum's education staff to design a workshop that looked at both the boiler and the adjacent glass box for refuse and recycling known as the "Trash Palace," built by Edge Studio (now GBBN), as a site for an environmentally responsive public art project. We invited a wide range of experts to participate, including leaders and emerging leaders in public art,

ANDREA POLLI

technology, environment, landscape architecture, and engineering. To help facilitate, I also brought a team of artists, technologists, and designers: Cecilia McKinnon, Eric Geusz, Isaiah Smith, and Matthew Barbato. Over four days, we toured the boiler, heard from scientists and engineers, and recorded images, sound, air quality, and other environmental data using devices including CREATE Lab's Speck and HabitatMap's Airbeam. We undertook an intensive boot camp based on the Stanford D-School's Design Thinking curriculum.

In teams, participants developed project concept proposals for the site, and through these visions, the boiler was given a new life befitting its potential role as an electricity generator. What follows are the resulting concept proposals—sometimes whimsical, occasionally personal, and often empowering. The participants found connections to energy in their community and formed bonds with their fellow team members, emphasizing the potential benefits of cross-disciplinary collaborations that respond to community environmental challenges.

Note

[1] Michael Chabon, *The Mysteries of Pittsburgh* (New York: William Morrow and Company, 1988), 50.

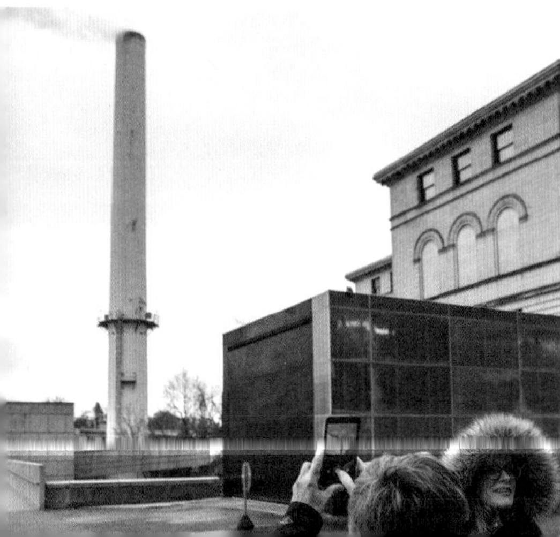


Service Enclosure (known colloquially as "the Trash Palace"), Carnegie Museums of Pittsburgh

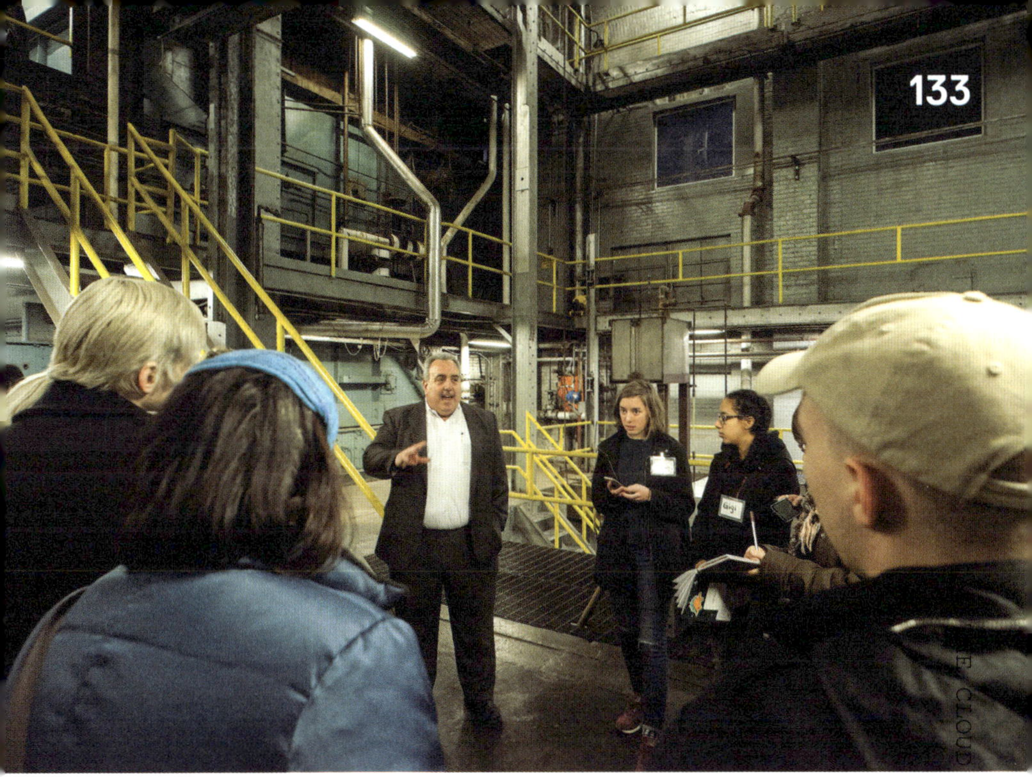

Tony Young, Vice President, Planning & Operations, Office of the Vice President, Carnegie Museums of Pittsburgh (above) and Bill Kubit, Plant Manager, Bellefield Boiler Plant (below) speaking with participants of the Cloud Factory Workshops

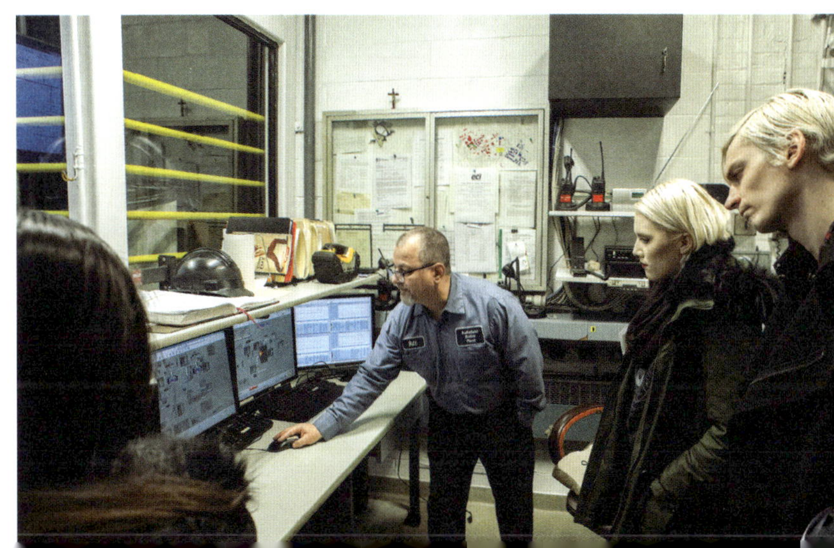

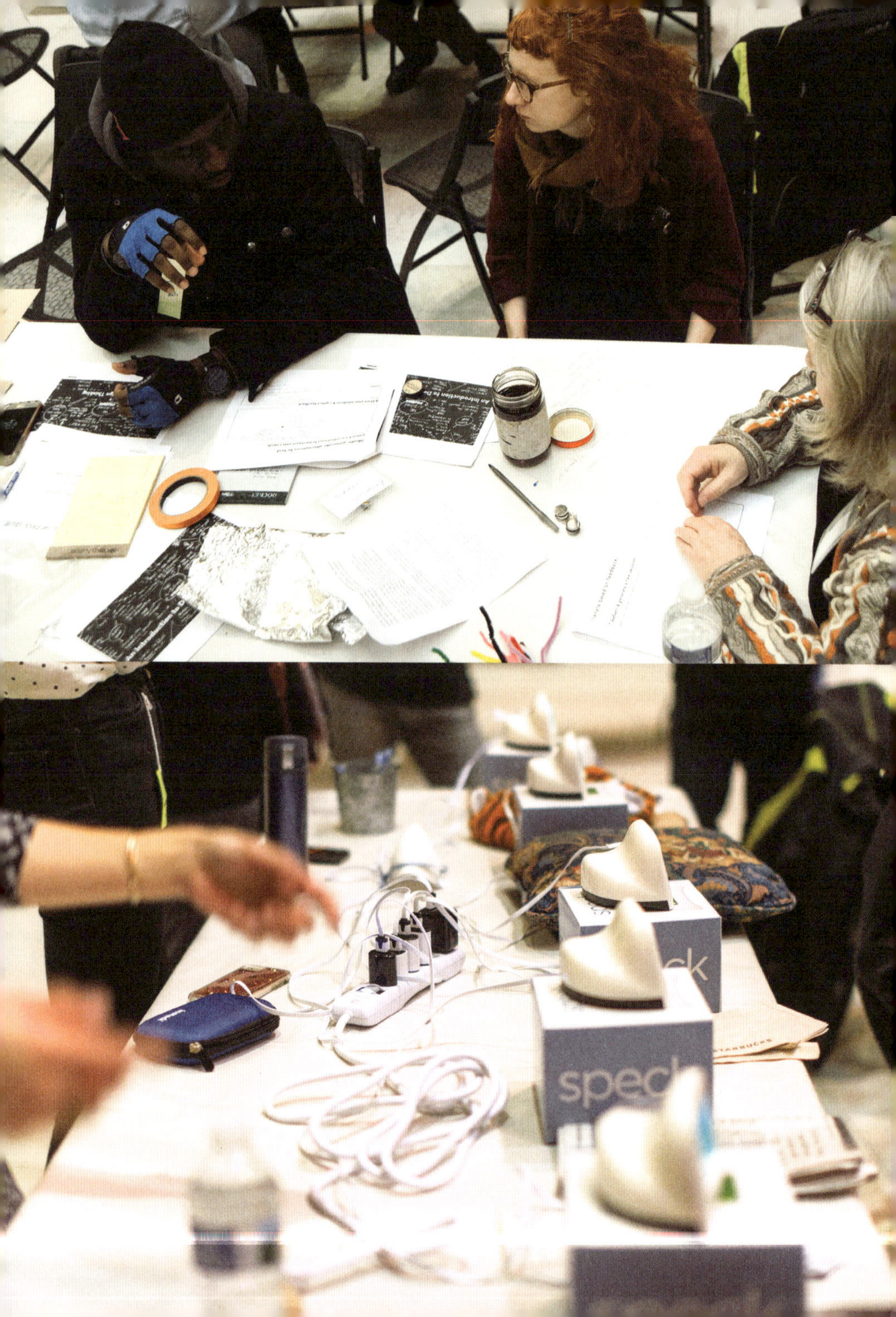

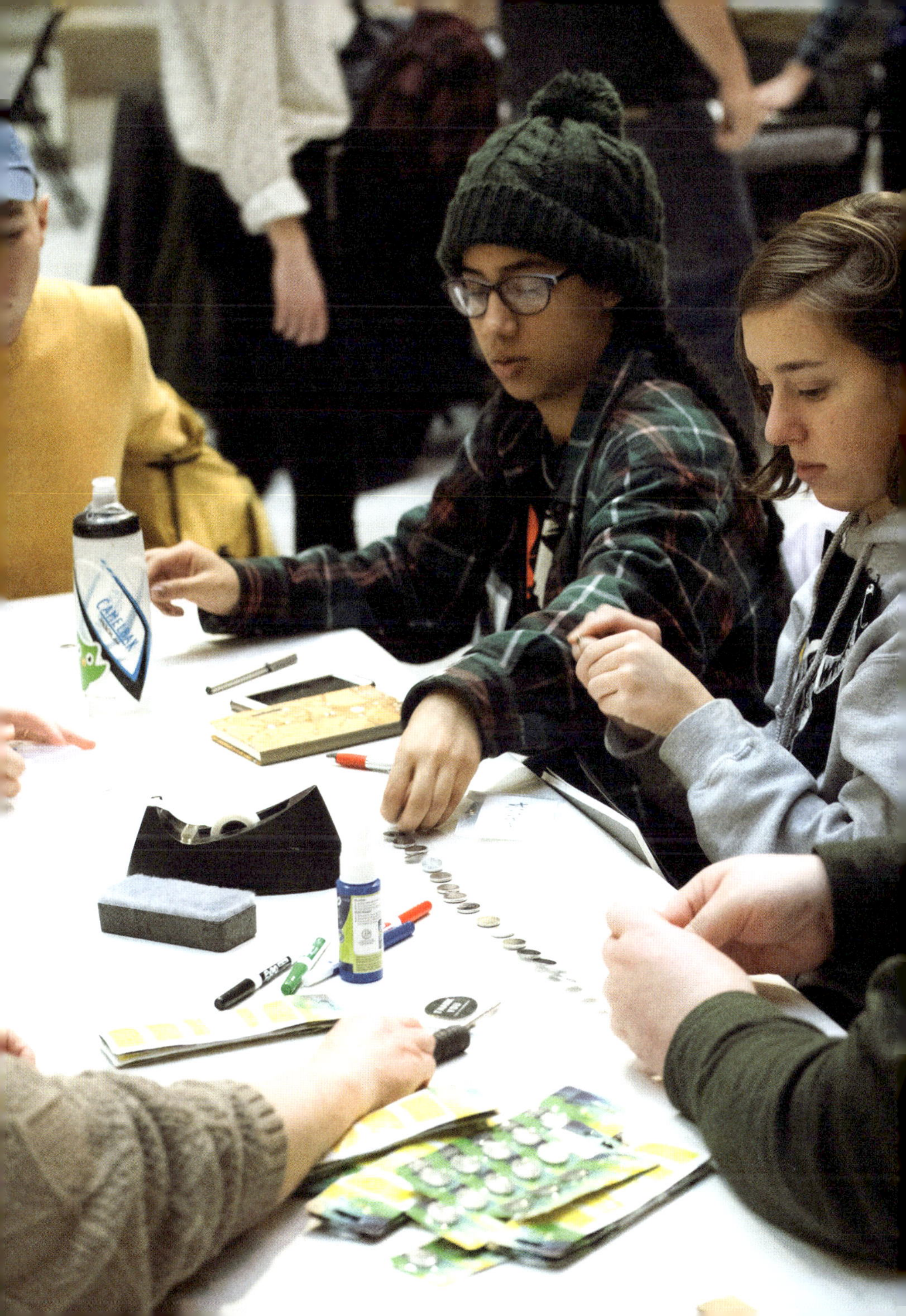

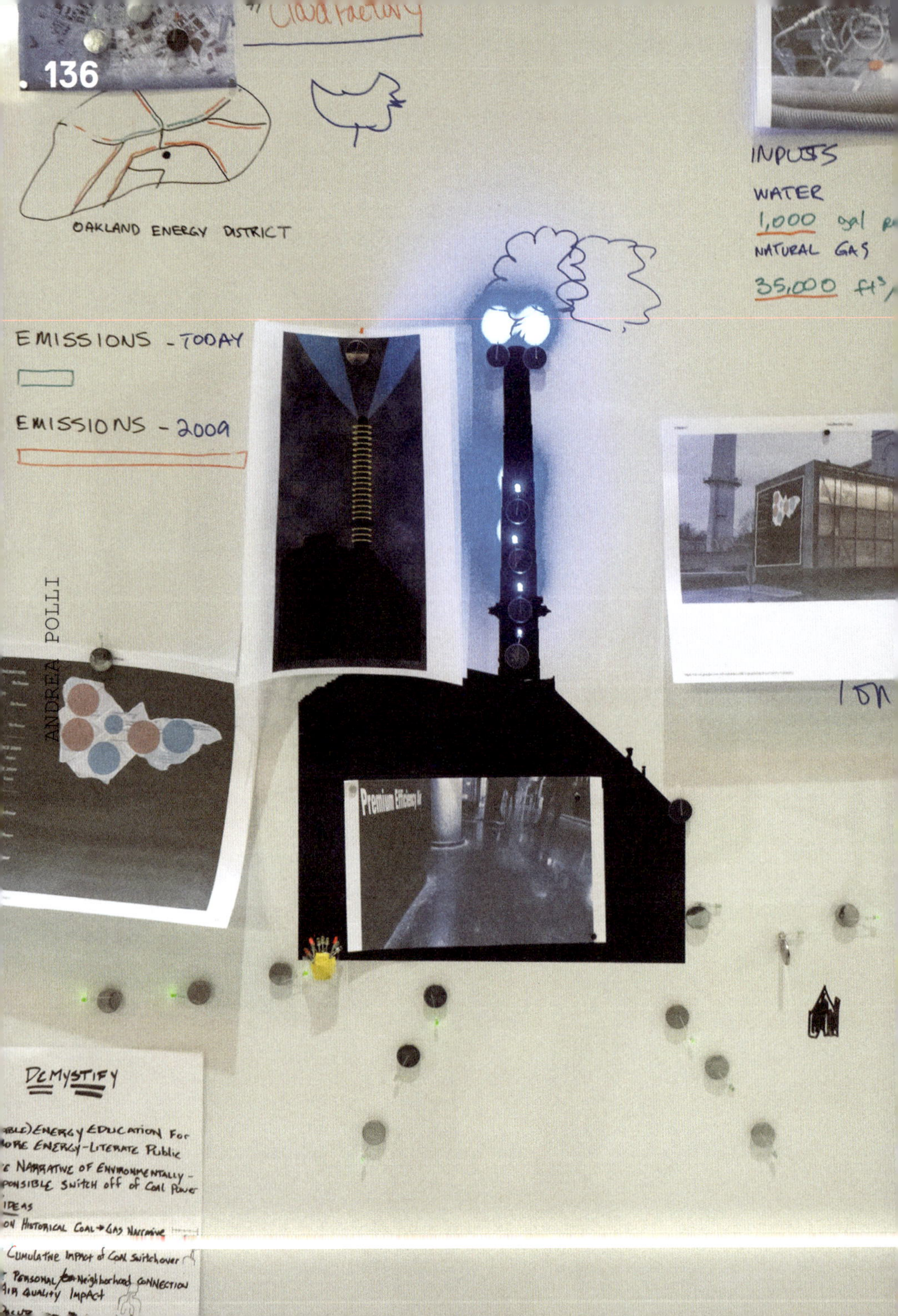
136
Cloud factory
OAKLAND ENERGY DISTRICT
INPUTS
WATER
1,000 gal R..
NATURAL GAS
35,000 ft³
EMISSIONS - TODAY
EMISSIONS - 2009
ANDREA POLLI
Premium Efficiency
DEMYSTIFY
BLE) ENERGY EDUCATION FOR
ORE ENERGY-LITERATE PUBLIC
E NARRATIVE OF ENVIRONMENTALLY-
PONSIBLE SWITCH OFF OF COAL POWER
IDEAS
ON HISTORICAL COAL → GAS NARRATIVE
Cumulative Impact of Coal switchover
Personal &/or Neighborhood CONNECTION
AIR QUALITY IMPACT

The Cloud Factory:
*Hack the Grid* Workshops
with Andrea Polli
January 2017


The following six projects suggest ways
to use the gas-fired Bellefield Boiler as
a site to help people understand data on
matters like pollution, energy, weather,
and climate. We typically lack visible proof
of the damage done by the environmental
impact of such everyday actions as flipping
a light switch. But what if each utility
had a corresponding work of art, seen
by everyone, that changed and morphed
with our usage?

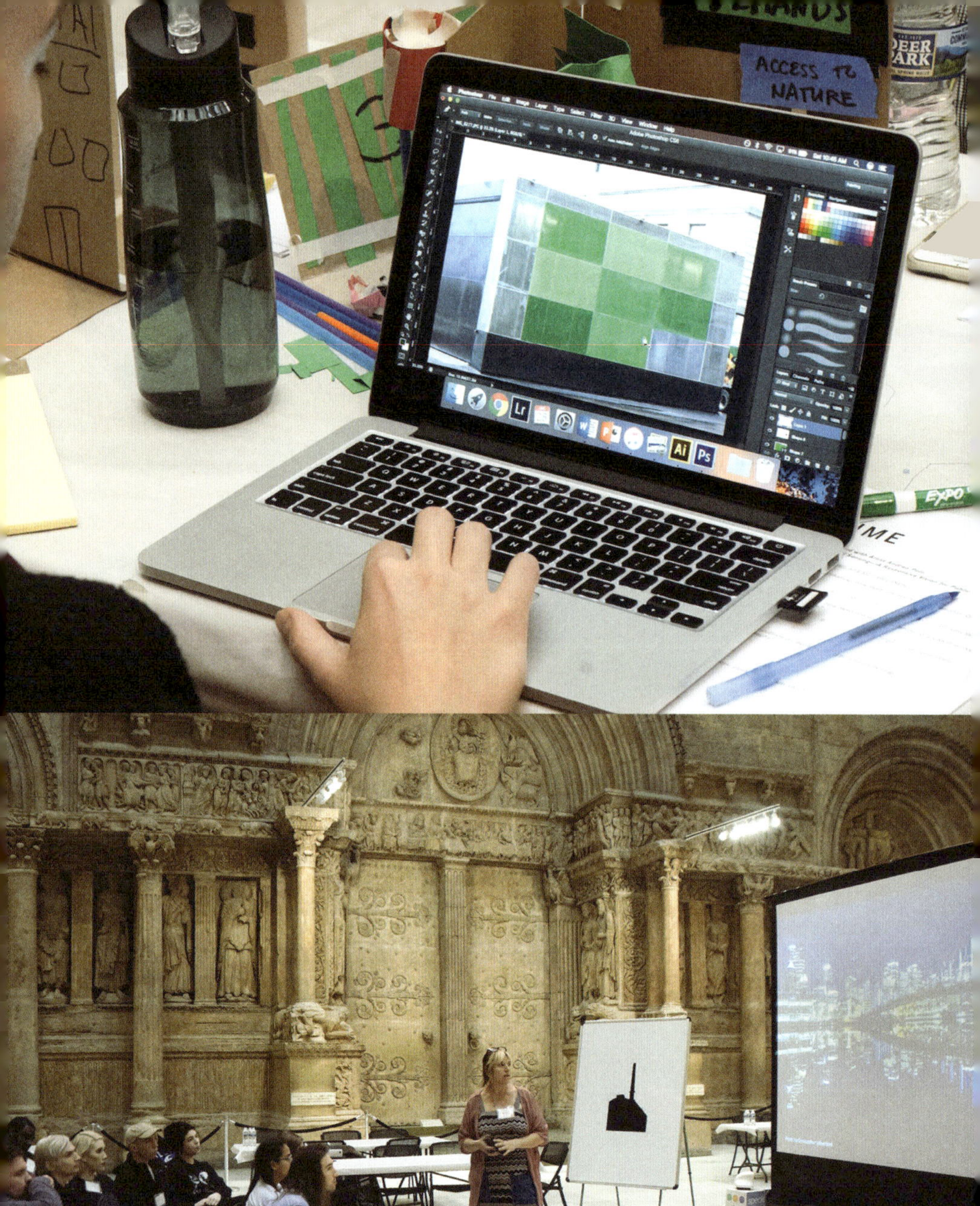
ACCESS TO
NATURE

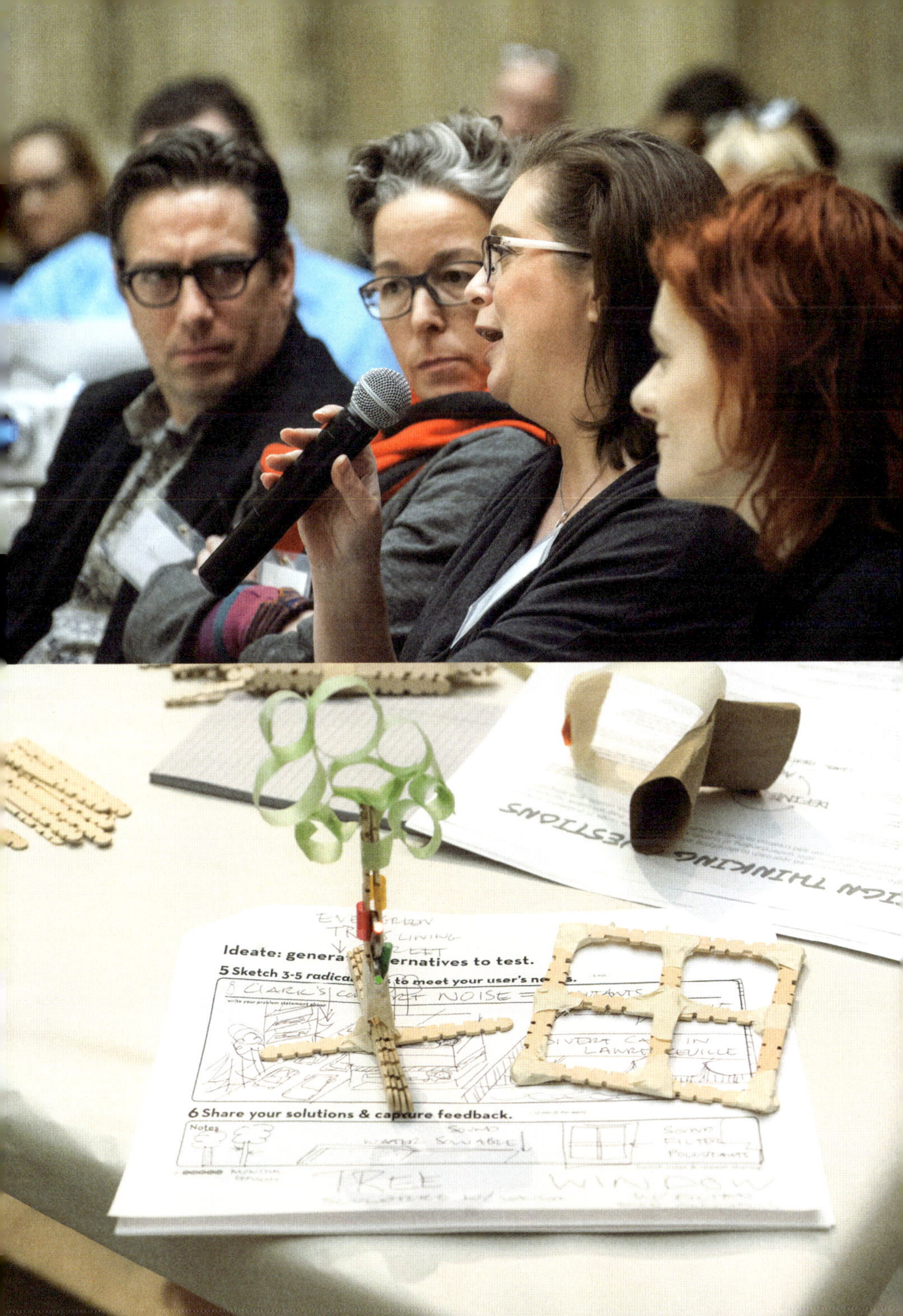
Ideate: genera... ...ernatives to test.
5 Sketch 3-5 radical ... to meet your user's ne...s.
CLARK'S
write your problem statement above
NOISE =
6 Share your solutions & capture feedback.
Notes
TREE
WINDOW
DESIGN THINKING QUESTIONS

# BELEAF

Project Team:
Racheljoy Rodas, Heather Mallak

**BELEAF conceptualizes indoor air quality monitoring objects for the home. These objects are designed to enable data sharing and networking with others, providing a platform for residents to make improvements across neighborhoods. These objects can be personalized—both aesthetically and programmatically— so that they can fold into one's daily life as well as highlight changes in the environment that are personally meaningful to the user.**

ANDREA POLLI

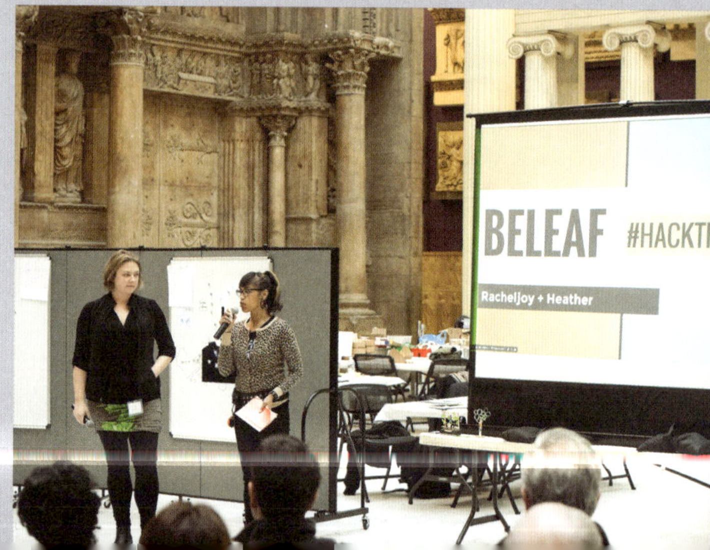

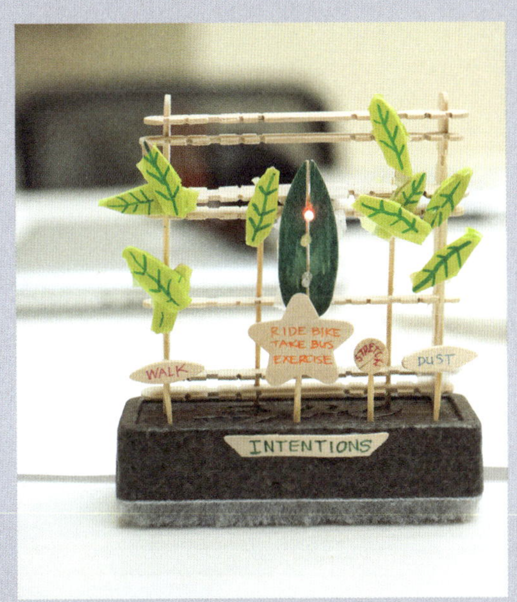
RIDE BIKE
TAKE BUS
EXERCISE
STRETCH
WALK
DUST
INTENTIONS

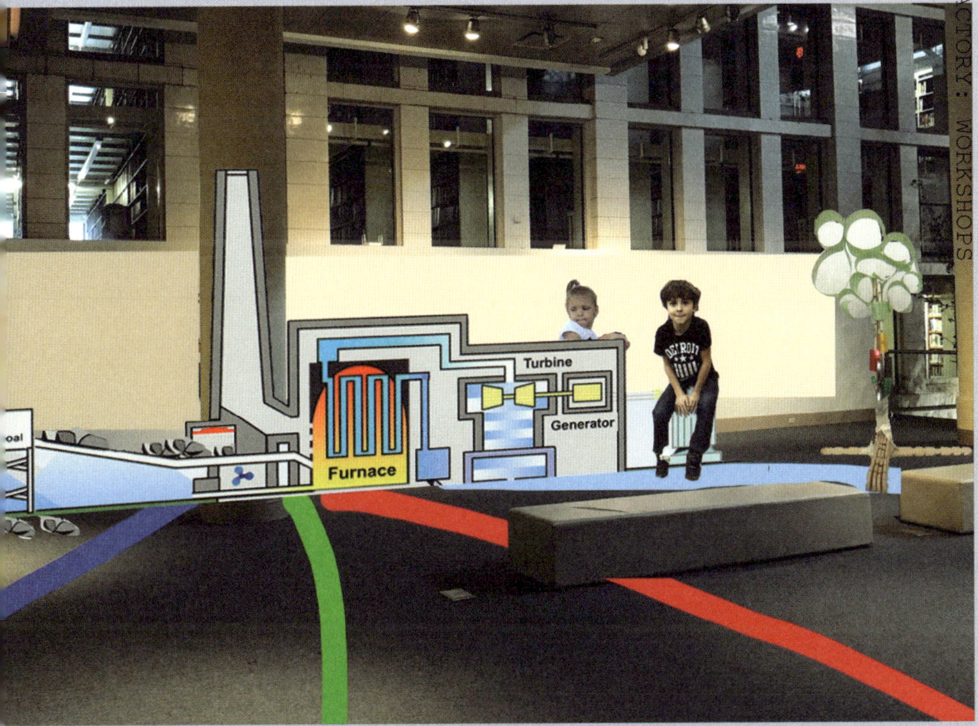

Coal
Turbine
Generator
Furnace
DETROIT

# The Bubble Factory

Project Team:
Nina Chase, Rebecca Popowsky,
Sam Barton, Carin Mincemoyer

ANDREA POLLI

The Bubble Factory is a playful installation that makes the Bellefield Boiler's energy consumption legible to neighborhood residents and visitors. Drawing inspiration from historic forms of long-distance visual communication such as smoke signals, the project proposes a contemporary and whimsical twist: bubbles! The density of bubbles billowing from the stack will directly correlate to energy produced and distributed by the plant in real time.

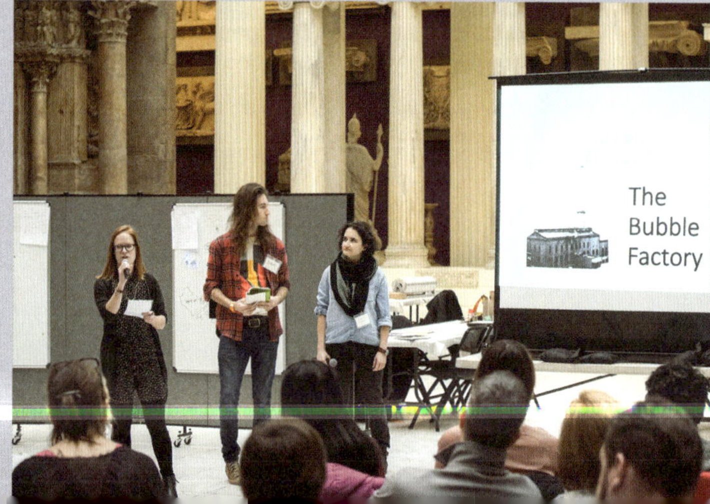

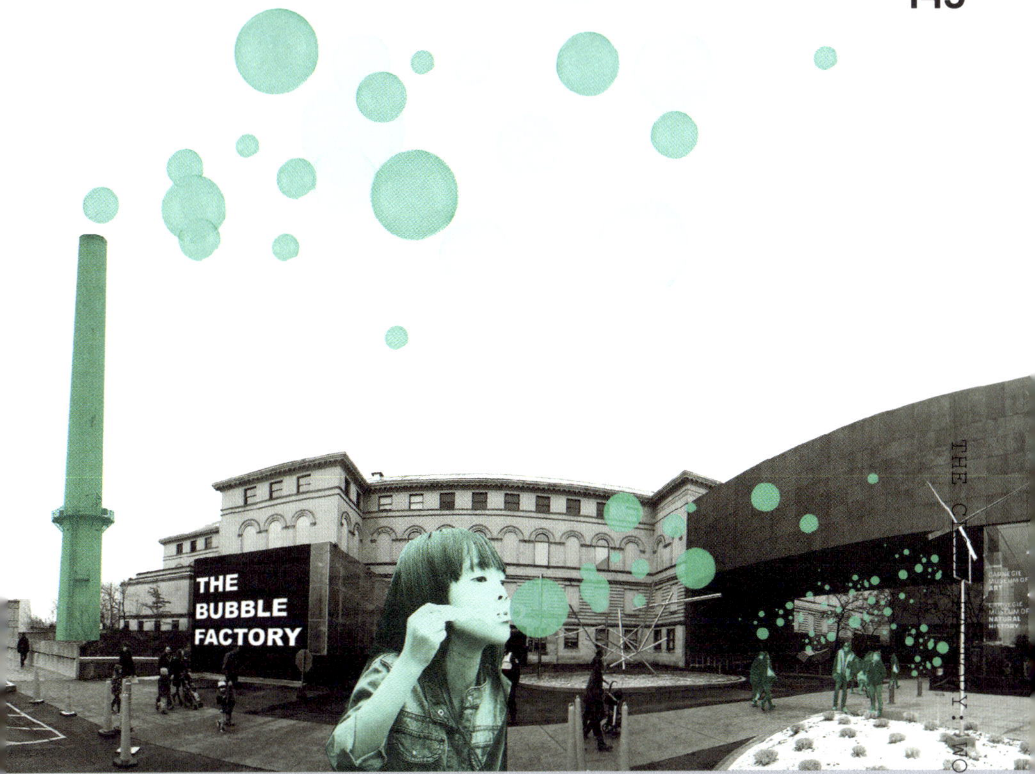

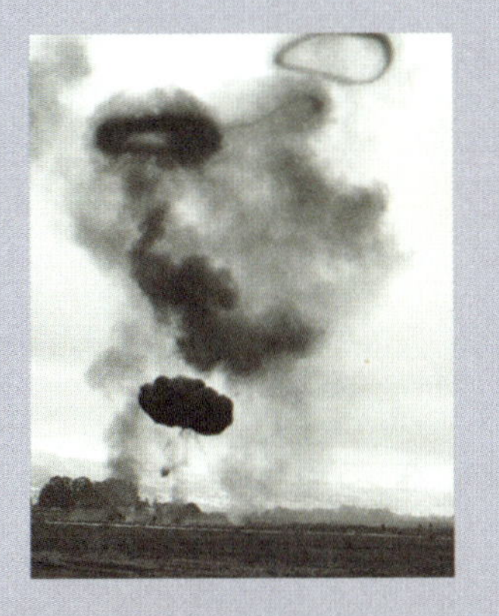

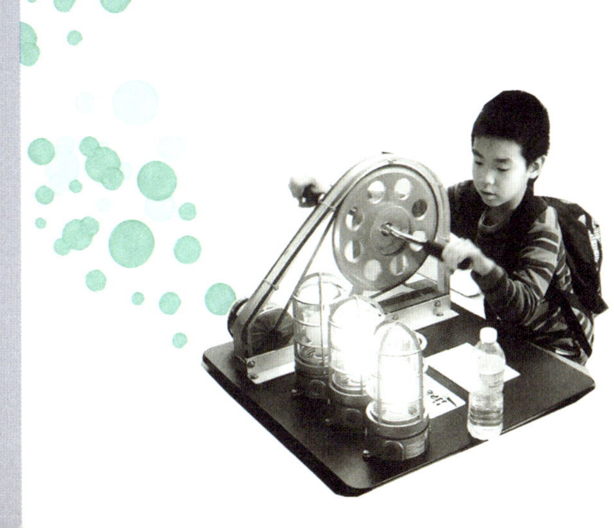
THE
BUBBLE
FACTORY

THE ______Y : WORKSHOPS

# Crowning the Trash Palace


Project Team:
Kirsi Jansa, Randy Hyland,
Andrea Maue, Laura Ramie


**Inspired by the recent conservation of *The Crowning of Labor*—which purposefully retained several small patches created by years of exposure to air pollution—this proposal adapts the mural's iconic imagery. On the facade of the museum's waste facility, known informally as the Trash Palace, sections of the mural would transform in response to local air quality, while a carbon clock and global thermometer remind us of our place in the global community.**



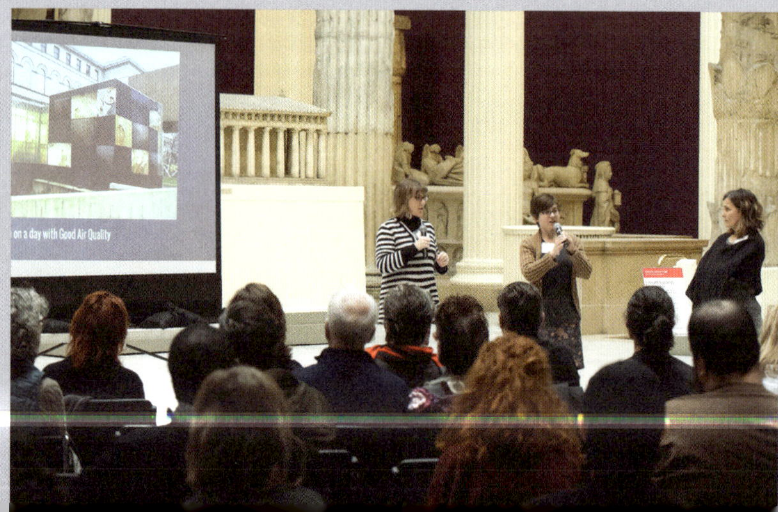

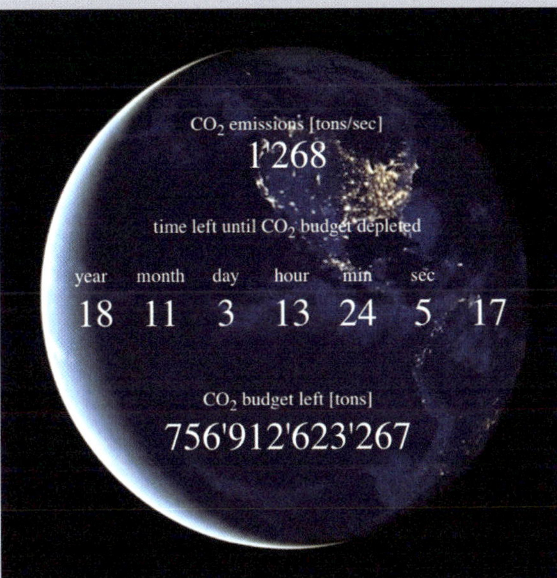
CO2 emissions [tons/sec]
1'268
time left until CO2 budget depleted
year   month   day   hour   min   sec
18   11   3   13   24   5   17
CO2 budget left [tons]
756'912'623'267

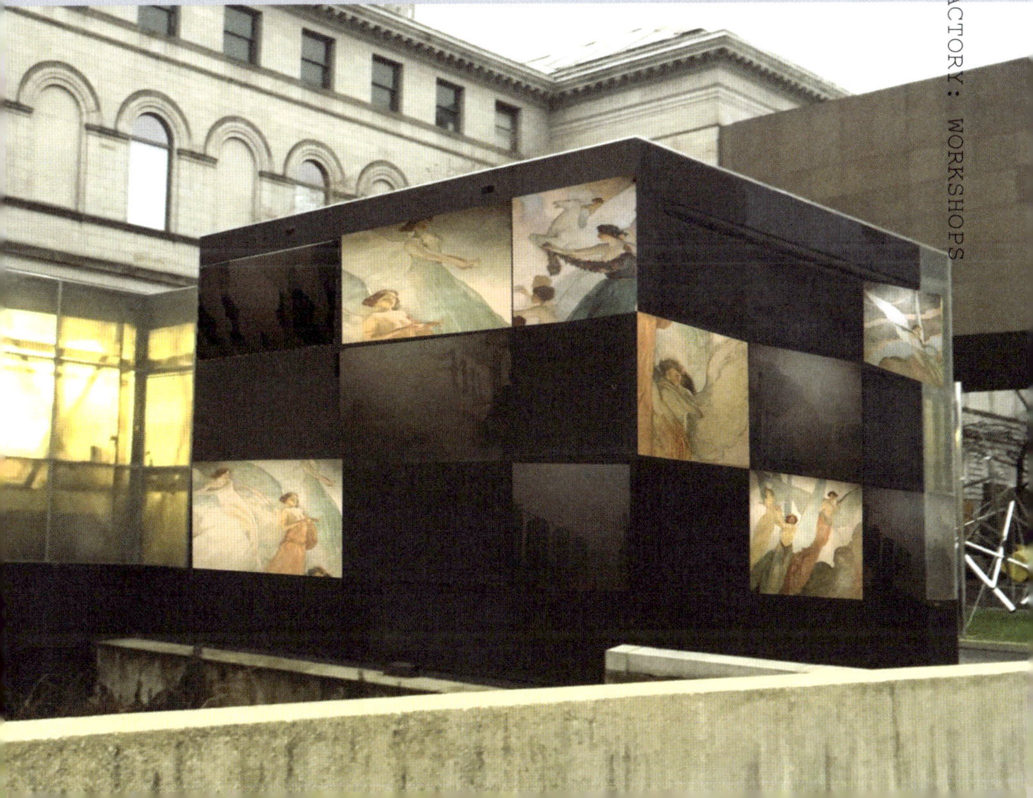

# Griddy


Project Team:
Teresa DeFlitch, Jessica Pachuta,
Patrick Yaber, Gigi Varlotta, Hanna Wells


ANDREA POLLI

In Griddy, graphic screens on the facade of the Trash Palace transform in response to pressure pads embedded in the ground outside. Each pad corresponds to a Pittsburgh site or institution powered by the Bellefield Boiler, and when you jump on a pressure pad, the steam output for that location appears on the facade. Between activations, the screens return to a resting state that features silhouettes of workers—a nod to Pittsburgh's industrial and labor histories.

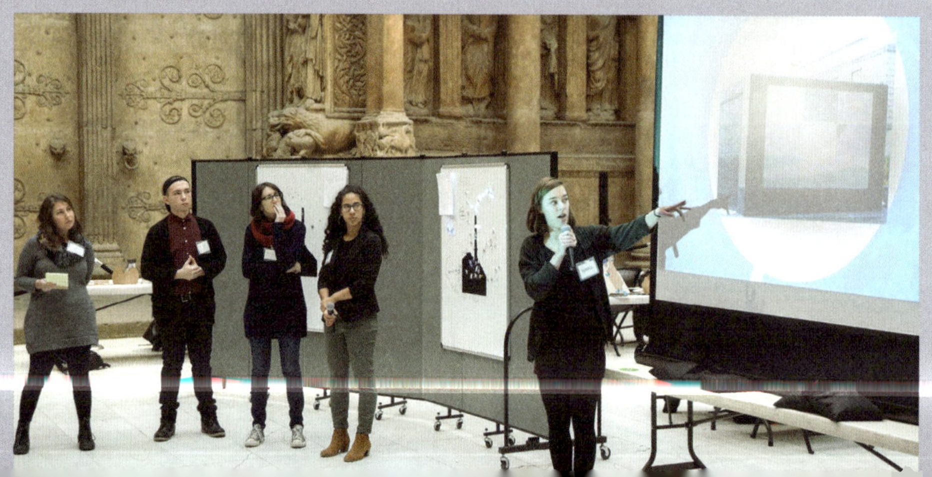

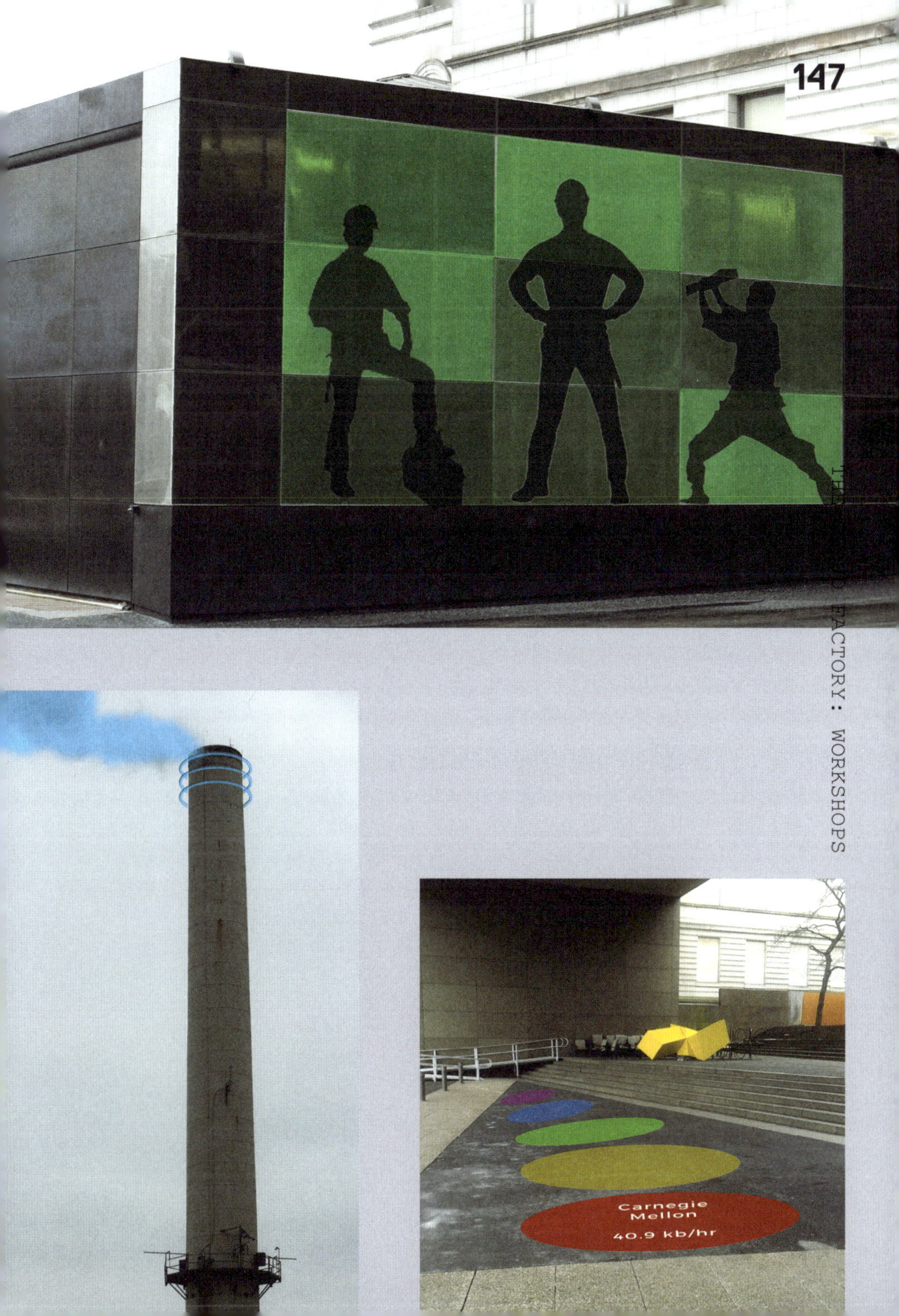

THE DISTRIBUTED FACTORY : WORKSHOPS
Carnegie
Mellon
40.9 kb/hr

# Particulate Literacy

Project Team:
Joshua Walls, Sam Milford,
Matthew Barbato

**Particulate Literacy empowers residents by providing easy access to information about local air quality. In locations where Pittsburghers often gather such as libraries and bus stops, these screens allow people to both access and share knowledge about the conditions in their local communities.**



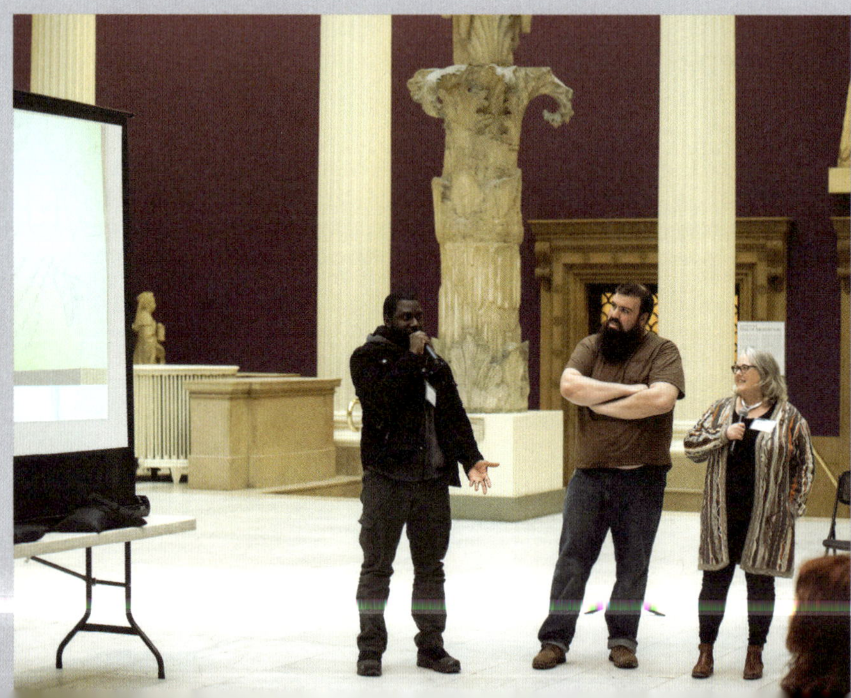

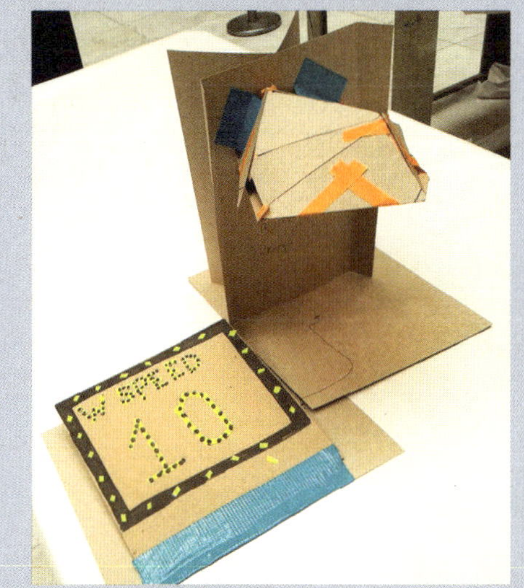
W SPEED
10

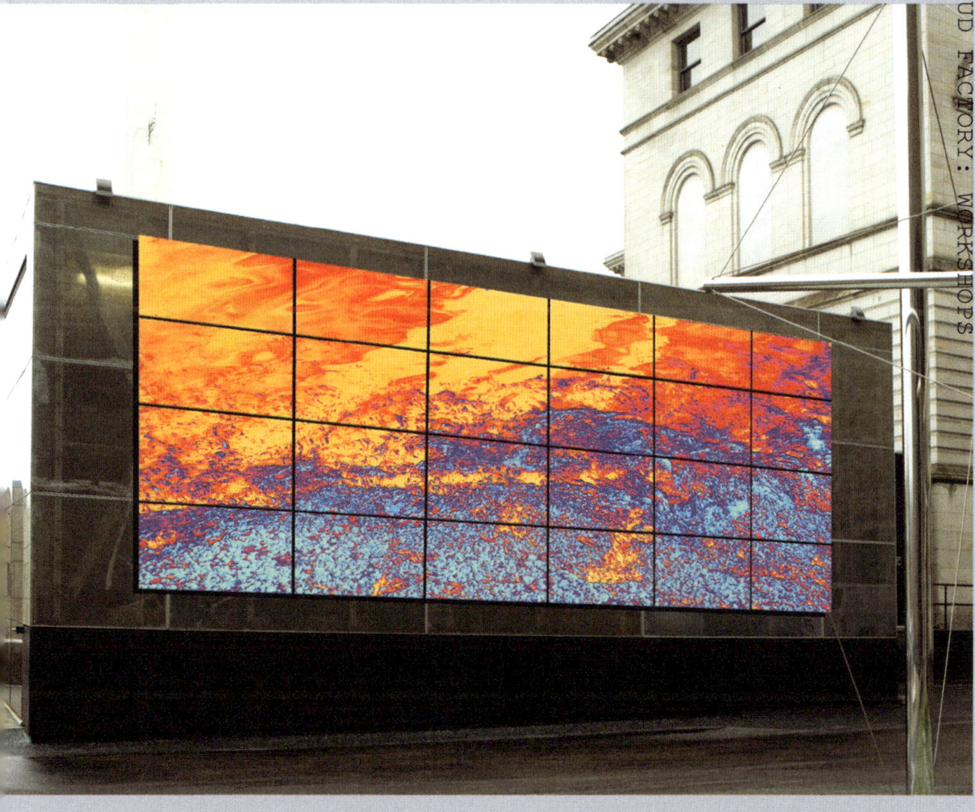

# Project Demystify


Project Team:
Angelos Tzelepis, Clarke Bacharach,
Eric Geusz


ANDREA POLLI

**Project Demystify dresses the smokestack of the Bellefield Boiler as a lighthouse. As a strong visual symbol for the community, this eye-catching art installation draws attention to the importance of clean energy in an age of rapid global warming. Paired with a dashboard that features information about the boiler, Project Demystify provides opportunities to learn more about energy consumption and the infrastructure that supports it.**

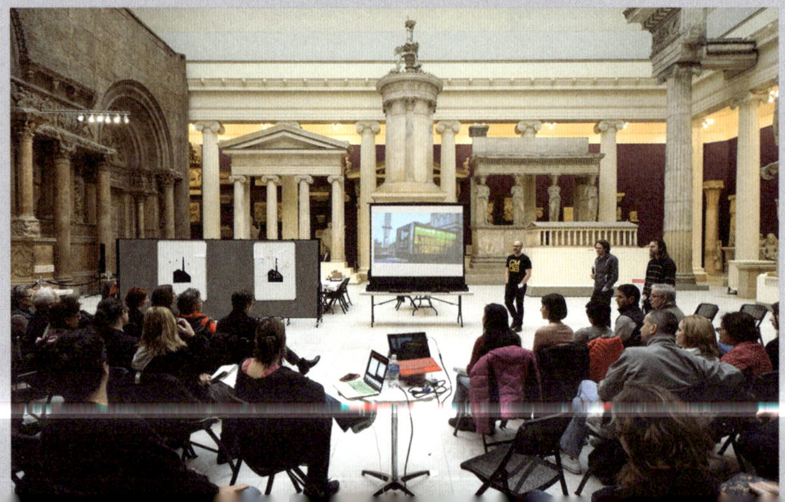

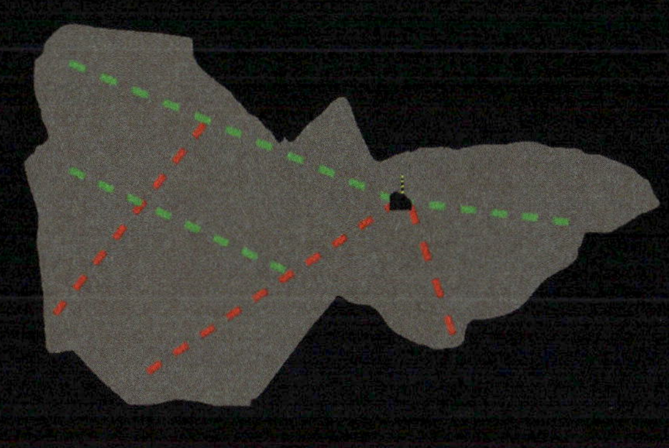

**CURRENT STEAM GENERATION**
267000 lb/hour

**EMISSIONS - CURRENT**
2000 lb/hour

**EMISSIONS - PRE-2009 SYSTEM**
13000 lb/hour

- - - - - - - - - - - - - - - - - - - - - - -

**WATER USAGE**
9593 gal/hour

**GAS USAGE**
35000 ft³/hour

**OIL USAGE (BACKUP SYSTEM)**
0 gal/hour

- - - - - - - - - - - - - - - - - - - - - - -

**WATER USAGE PER PERSON**
10.46 gal/day

**GASOLINE EQUIVALENT PER PERSON**
.508 gal/day

**EMMISSIONS PER PERSON**
1.12 lb/day

In 2009, the Bellefield Boiler Plant was converted from coal furnaces with natural gas backup to gas furnaces with oil backup.

This conversion has greatly reduced emissions of pollutants and improved the air quality in Oakland and the surrounding neighborhoods.

**COAL NOT BURNED SINCE 2009**
166789 tons

**EMISSIONS SAVED SINCE 2009**
4658743 tons

**LIVES SAVED SINCE 2009**
736



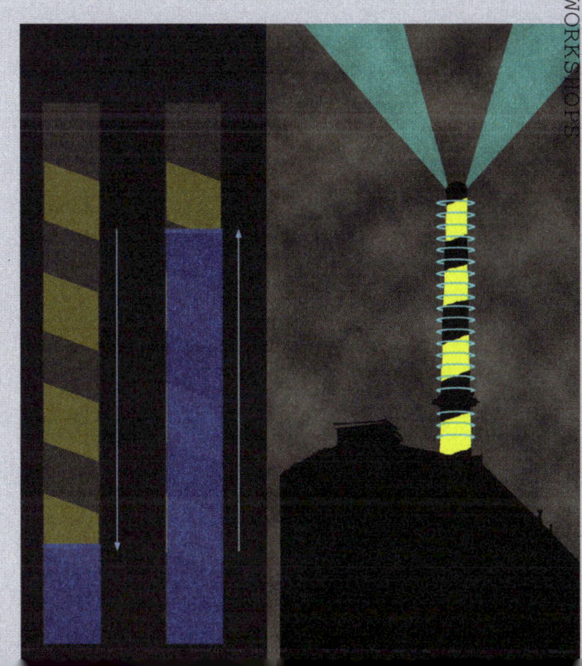

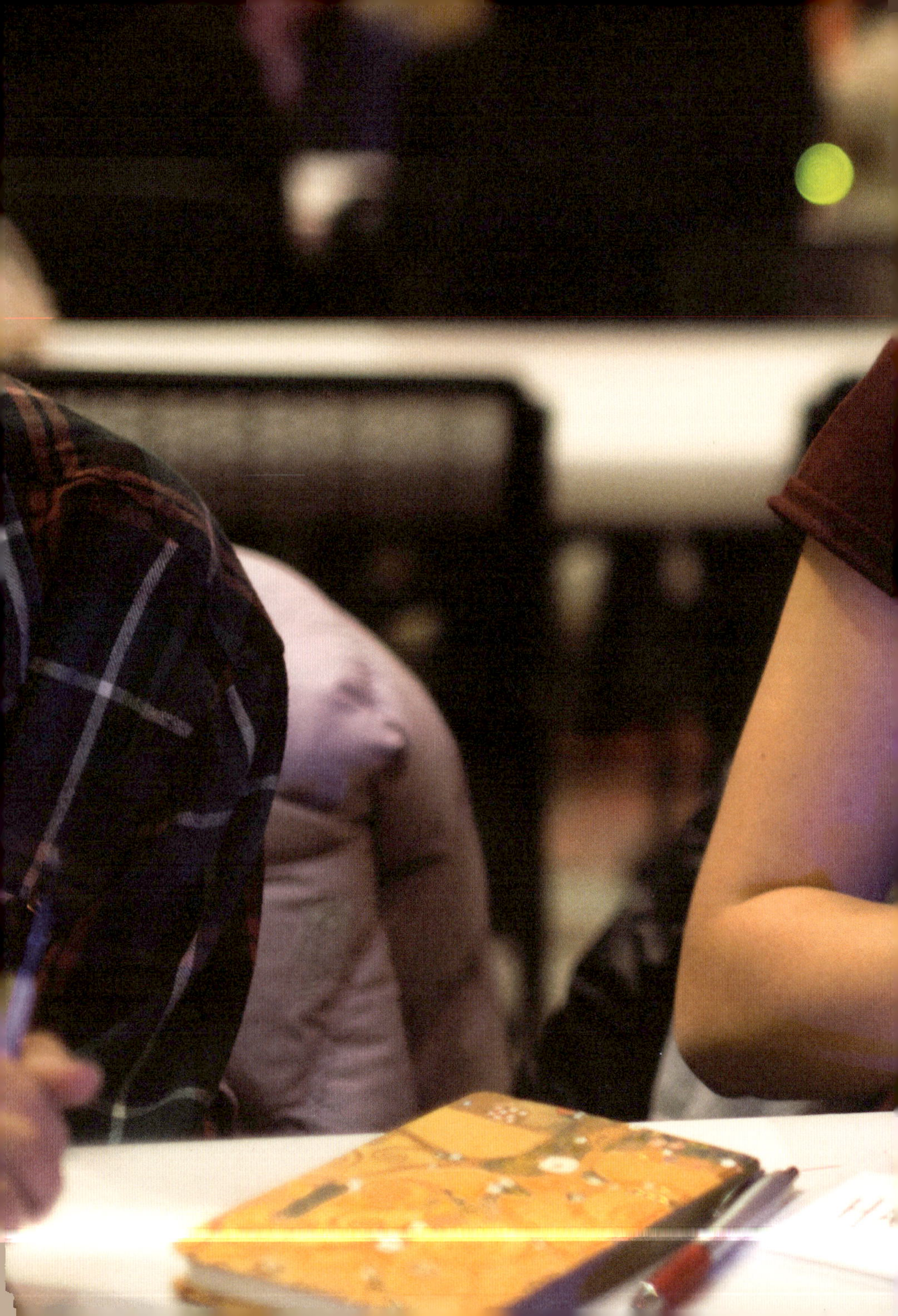

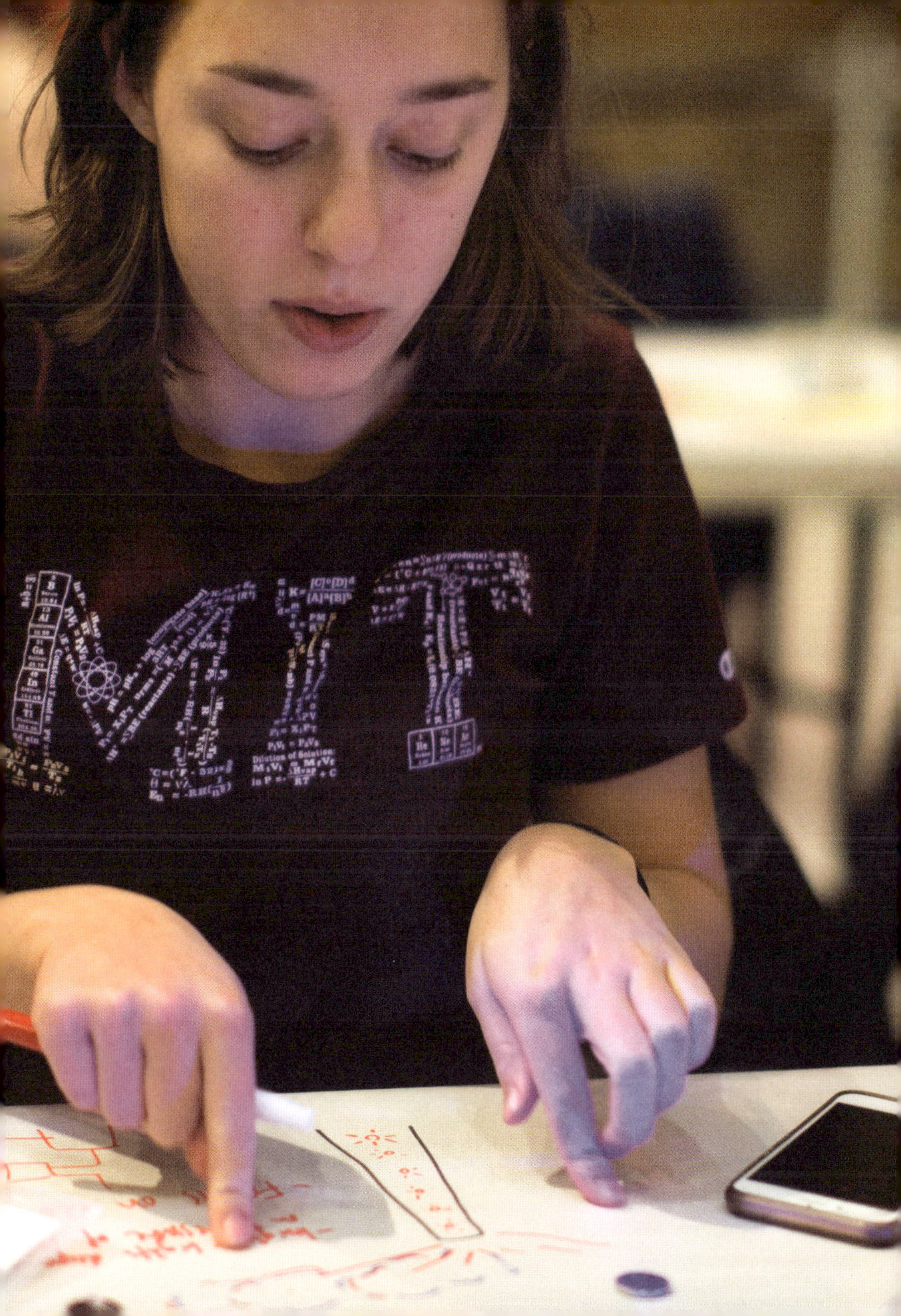

# Keep on Hacking
the Grid

ANDREA POLLI

The projects in this book only scratch the surface of what might be possible when you know more about your energy systems and how to engage with the impacts of that energy on multiple levels. Both as an individual and as part of a larger group of like-minded thinkers, you can adapt your skills and interests to make positive changes in your own community. Did you find motivation in the work of Allegheny County Clean Air Now, who mixed observation, technology, and occasionally even performance to effect change? You can form a clean air action group in your neighborhood, using social media and other digital tools to share important information.

Are you more comfortable with electronics and programming? Take inspiration from CREATE Lab and activate your skills to gather and organize images and other data to help communities advocate for a cleaner environment. Do you identify with the artists and designers who participated in the Cloud Factory workshops? Develop and pitch a proposal to transform something in your own neighborhood from an eyesore to a compelling work of public art. Whatever your interests or expertise, as an energy consumer empowered by information, there is no end to what you can "hack" when the goal is to make positive change and render visible something that might be otherwise unseen.

**156**

For her creative vision, collaborative spirit, and commitment to environmental sustainability, Carnegie Museum of Art and the Hillman Photography Initiative wish to acknowledge and thank Andrea Polli. Her public art in Pittsburgh has engaged audiences at a grand scale and contributed to both the cultural and civic life of our city. We hope that the projects and writing in *Hack the Grid* will encourage its readers to adapt image-making technologies toward meaningful actions in their own communities.

The museum would also like to thank the many people with whom we collaborated to develop and realize the workshops, projects, and installations that occurred in Pittsburgh throughout 2016 and 2017.

We thank especially our workshop leaders:

| | |
|---|---|
| Matthew Barbato | Cecilia McKinnon |
| Eric Geusz | Isaiah Smith |

For their role in the workshops and participation in this catalogue, we thank the Community Robotics, Education, and Technology Empowerment Lab (CREATE Lab) of Carnegie Mellon University, including:

| | |
|---|---|
| Beatrice Dias | Sara Longo |
| Paul Dille | Illah Nourbakhsh |
| Ryan Hoffmann | Randy Sargent |
| Yen-Chia Hsu | |

We also thank the additional workshop presenters, tour leaders, and respondents, including:

| | |
|---|---|
| Dee Briggs | Alison Langmead |
| Lori Hepner | Dutch MacDonald |
| Bill Kubit | Albert Presto |

We are especially grateful to the many people whose participation in the workshops contributed to their success:

| | |
|---|---|
| Clarke Bacharach | Jonathan Greene |
| Sam Barton | Randy Hyland |
| Mary Boening | Kirsi Jansa |
| Nina Chase | Heather Mallak |
| Teresa DeFlitch | Andrea Maue |

ACKNOWLEDGMENTS

Sam Milford
Carin Mincemoyer
Jessica Pachuta
Lynn Pellegrino
Raquel Peterson
Rebecca Popowsky
Laura Ramie
Matt Reiser

Racheljoy Rodas
Dameta Skinner
Angelos Tzelepis
Gigi Varlotta
Joshua Walls
Hanna Wells
Patrick Yaber

For their support, input, and encouragement, we thank:
The Greater Pittsburgh Arts Council
The Land Art Generator Initiative (LAGI)
Allegheny County Clean Air Now (ACCAN)

Leah Andrascik
Robert Ferry
Elizabeth Monoian

Thaddeus Popovich
Jennifer Saffron

For their role in facilitating research trips and bringing their insight to these projects, we also thank:

Brian Cohen
Neil Donahue
Anna Johnson

Sallyann Kluz
Joel Tarr

The creativity, experience, and resourcefulness of the staff of Carnegie Museums of Pittsburgh were essential in realizing Andrea Polli's goals for these projects. Our thanks go out to everyone, and we wish to especially acknowledge members of the curatorial, education, facilities, and publications departments, and the Powdermill Nature Reserve:

Bryan Conley
Luke DeGroote
Catherine Evans
Tom Fisher
Natalia Gomez
Divya Rao Heffley
Andrea Kautz
Dan Leers
Cokie Lindsay
Bob Miller

Laurel Mitchell
Matthew Newton
Greg Paulowski
Mary Shidel
Jake Slyder
Marilyn Russell
Lucy Stewart
John Wenzel
Tony Young

**158**

ACKNOWLEDGMENTS

This book would not have been possible without the many people who offered their time and talents, including:
Philip R. S. Johnson of The Heinz Endowments, contributor
David B. Olsen, editor
Katie Reilly, former director of publishing for the museum
Brett Yasko, designer

For providing support for *Energy Flow*, *Particle Falls*, and *Hack the Grid*, we wish to thank:
Covestro
Riverlife
The City of Pittsburgh
The Pittsburgh Downtown Partnership
DQE Communications
Duquesne Light
Ron Gdovic and Mark Goyke of WindStax
Sargent Electric
Chris Clavio of Clavion Unlimited
Eric Geusz and Jared Rendon-Trompak
    of The Social Media Workgroup
The Compton Foundation
The Heinz Endowments's Breathe Project
The Pittsburgh Office of Public Art
The Pittsburgh Cultural Trust
The University of New Mexico
    College of Fine Arts, Department of Art
    Center for Advanced Research Computing
    Mesa Del Sol Endowment
    Americorps/VISTA, STEAM New Mexico

Finally, we wish to thank you—all of you. Your interaction and engagement with *Hack the Grid* are not only vital to the project itself, but are also fundamental to the strength of our communities and the future of our environment. As Andrea Polli writes here, "You are made of energy and have the power."

**A Special Note of Thanks:**
This important experimental program would not have been
possible without the generosity of the William Talbott Hillman
Foundation and the Henry L. Hillman Foundation. We are
especially grateful to Bill Hillman, who has championed
Carnegie Museum of Art's efforts to establish the Initiative
as a center for innovative thinking about the photographic
image. His dedication and support have been indispensable.

This publication is a project of LIGHTIME, a year of programming from Carnegie Museum of Art's Hillman Photography Initiative.

Divya Rao Heffley, Senior Program Manager, Hillman Photography Initiative

Natalia Gomez, Special Project Assistant, Hillman Photography Initiative

Agents, Hillman Photography Initiative: Liz Deschenes, Steffani Jemison, Dan Leers, and Laura Wexler

cmoa.org/lightime

Support for the Hillman Photography Initiative is provided by the William Talbott Hillman Foundation and the Henry L. Hillman Foundation. General operating support for Carnegie Museum of Art is provided by The Heinz Endowments and Allegheny Regional Asset District. Carnegie Museum of Art receives state arts funding support through a grant from the Pennsylvania Council on the Arts, a state agency funded by the Commonwealth of Pennsylvania.

Designed by Brett Yasko

Edited by David B. Olsen, Katie Reilly, and Matthew Newton

Photo research by Laurel Mitchell

Printed in Canada by The Prolific Group

ISBN 978-0-88039-061-3

Library of Congress Cataloging-in-Publication Data
Names: Polli, Andrea. | Johnson, Philip R. S.
Title: Hack the grid / Andrea Polli ; with contribution Philip R. S. Johnson.
Description: Pittsburgh, Pennsylvania : Carnegie Museum of Art, 2017. |
Includes bibliographical references.
Identifiers: LCCN 2017045089 |
ISBN 9780880390613 (alk. paper)
Subjects: LCSH: Art and technology—Pennsylvania—Pittsburgh—History—21st century. | Art and social action Pennsylvania—Pittsburgh—History—21st century. | Art, American—Pennsylvania—Pittsburgh—21st century—Themes, motives.
Classification: LCC N72.T4 H33 2017 |
DDC 700.1/05—dc23 LC record available at lccn.loc.gov/2017045089



Published by
Carnegie Museum of Art
4400 Forbes Avenue
Pittsburgh, Pennsylvania, 15213–4080
cmoa.org

Available through D.A.P./
Distributed Art Publishers
155 Sixth Avenue, 2nd Floor
New York, New York 10013
artbook.com

Image Credits
Every reasonable attempt has been made to identify and ensure accurate credit information for the images in this book. Any errors or omissions will be corrected in future editions.

p. 46: Subhankar Banerjee; pp. 59–60: Courtesy the Breathe Project; p. 128: Images courtesy Carnegie Museum of Art, Pittsburgh; p. 143: Courtesy of Nina Chase, Rebecca Popowsky, Sam Barton, and Carin Mincemoyer; pp. 6–9, 18–19, 22–23, 26–28, 35, 36 (top), 38–38, 80–82, 85–86, 91, 98–99, 101, 118–19, 124–27, 132–36, 138–40, 141 (top), 142, 144, 146, 148, 150: Bryan Conley; pp. 63, 93–94: Courtesy Carnegie Mellon University CREATE Lab and Allegheny County Clean Air Now (ACCAN); p. 147: Courtesy Teresa DeFlitch, Jessica Pachuta, Patrick Yaber, Gigi Varlotta, and Hanna Wells; p. 53: Eric Geusz; p. 145 (bottom): Courtesy Kirsi Jansa, Randy Hyland, Andrea Maue, and Laura Ramie; p. 82: Lynn Johnson; p. 43: Mark Lee Koven; p. 104–5: Christopher Litherland; p. 145 (top): Screenshot of carbon clock, Mercator Research Institute on Global Commons and Climate Change; pp. 47, 69 (bottom left), 74–75, 78–79, 107: Andrea Polli; p. 141 (bottom): Courtesy Racheljoy Rodas and Heather Mallack; pp. 2, 20–21, 134 (bottom), 152–3: Isaiah Smith; pp. 4–5 10–17, 30–31, 34, 36 (bottom), 45, 50, 54–56, 65, 66–67, 69 (top right), 70–73, 102–3, 108–9, 111–17, 120–21, 154–55: Jared Rendon Trompak; p. 151: Courtesy Angelos Tselepis, Clarke Bacharach, Eric Geuss; p. 149: Courtesy Joshua Walls, Sam Milford, and Matthew Barbato

**HILLMAN**PHOTOGRAPHY**INITIATIVE**
CARNEGIE MUSEUM OF **ART**